# Voicing the Voiceless

## Contributions to Closing Gaps
## in Cameroon History, 1958-2009

## Walter Gam Nkwi

**Langaa Research & Publishing CIG**
Mankon, Bamenda

Publisher:
*Langaa* RPCIG
Langaa Research & Publishing Common Initiative Group
P.O. Box 902 Mankon
Bamenda
North West Region
Cameroon
Langaagrp@gmail.com
www.langaa-rpcig.net


Distributed outside N. America by African Books Collective
orders@africanbookscollective.com
www.africanbookscollective.com


Distributed in N. America by Michigan State University Press
msupress@msu.edu
www.msupress.msu.edu


ISBN: 9956-616-40-0

DISCLAIMER

All views expressed in this publication are those of the author and do not necessarily reflect the views of Langaa RPCIG.

# Other Titles by *Langaa* RPCIG

**Tah Asongwed**
Born to Rule: Autobiography of a life President
Child of Earth

**Frida Menkan Mbunda**
Shadows From The Abyss

**Bongasu Tanla Kishani**
A Basket of Kola Nuts
Konglanjo (Spears of Love without Ill-fortune) and Letters to
Ethiopia with some Random Poems

**Fo Angwafo III S.A.N of Mankon**
Royalty and Politics: The Story of My Life

**Basil Diki**
The Lord of Anomy
Shrouded Blessings

**Churchill Ewumbue-Monono**
Youth and Nation-Building in Cameroon: A Study of National
Youth Day Messages and Leadership Discourse (1949-2009)

**Emmanuel N. Chia, Joseph C. Suh & Alexandre Ndeffo Tene**
Perspectives on Translation and Interpretation in Cameroon

**Linus T. Asong**
The Crown of Thorns
No Way to Die
A Legend of the Dead: Sequel of *The Crown of Thorns*
The Akroma File
Salvation Colony: Sequel to *No Way to Die*
Chopchair
Doctor Frederick Ngenito

**Vivian Sihshu Yenika**
Imitation Whiteman
Press Lake Varsity Girls: The Freshman Year

**Beatrice Fri Bime**
Someplace, Somewhere
Mystique: A Collection of Lake Myths

**Shadrach A. Ambanasom**
Son of the Native Soil
The Cameroonian Novel of English Expression:
An Introduction
**Tangie Nsoh Fonchingong and Gemandze John Bobuin**
Cameroon: The Stakes and Challenges of Governance and
Development

**Tatah Mentan**
Democratizing or Reconfiguring Predatory Autocracy? Myths and
Realities in Africa Today

**Roselyne M. Jua & Bate Besong**
To the Budding Creative Writer: A Handbook

**Albert Mukong**
Prisonner without a Crime: Disciplining Dissent in Ahidjo's
Cameroon

**Mbuh Tennu Mbuh**
In the Shadow of my Country

**Bernard Nsokika Fonlon**
Genuine Intellectuals: Academic and Social Responsibilities of
Universities in Africa

**Lilian Lem Atanga**
Gender, Discourse and Power in the Cameroonian Parliament

**Cornelius Mbifung Lambi & Emmanuel Neba Ndenecho**
Ecology and Natural Resource Development
in the Western Highlands of Cameroon: Issues in Natural Resource
Managment

**Gideon F. For-mukwai**
Facing Adversity with Audacity

**Peter W. Vakunta & Bill F. Ndi**
Nul n'a le monopole du français : deux poètes du Cameroon
anglophone

**Emmanuel Matateyou**
Les murmures de l'harmattan

**Ekpe Inyang**
The Hill Barbers

**JK Bannavti**
Rock of God *(Kilán ke Nyüy)*

**Godfrey B. Tangwa (Rotcod Gobata)**
I Spit on their Graves: Testimony Relevant to the Democratization
Struggle in Cameroon

**Henrietta Mambo Nyamnjoh**
"We Get Nothing from Fishishing", Fishing for Boat Opportunies
amongst Senegalese Fisher Migrants

**Bill F. Ndi, Dieurat Clervoyant & Peter W. Vakunta**
Les douleurs de la plume noire : du Cameroun anglophone à Haïti

**Laurence Juma**
Kileleshwa: A Tale of Love, Betrayal and Corruption in Kenya

**Nol Alembong**
Forest Echoes (Poems)

**Marie-Hélène Mottin-Sylla & Joëlle Palmieri**
Excision : les jeunes changent l'Afriaque par le TIC

**Walter Gam Nkwi**
Voicing the Voiceless: Contributions to Closing Gaps in
Cameroon History, 1958-2009

# Content

## Chapter Three

## Chapter Four

## Chapter Five

## Chapter Six

## Chapter Seven

## Chapter Eight

# Acknowledgements

It is often said amongst the Bamenda Grassfielders that one hand no matter how strong it is cannot tie a bundle. This simply means that many hands are needed in one way or the other before any meaningful thing is done. In that regard I want to acknowledge the fact that I am heavily indebted to many people who have helped me, directly or indirectly, individually or collectively, to make this work see the light of day. Given my extended and extensive networks, I am afraid that I cannot list all the names here. I am particularly indebted to my informants, without whom most parts of this work would never have been realised. The archivist, Prince Henry Mbain, who passed away in 2008, was a critical source and informant for over ten years before his death. In a special way, I am most grateful to Professors Piet Konings and Francis Nyamnjoh, for guidance, insights and very important comments on earlier drafts of this work. To all those who have contributed tremendously, and whom I haven't mentioned by name, I say thank you.

# Chapter One

## Introduction

This book is an endeavour to write the history of the voiceless in Africa with particular emphasis on Cameroon. This is on the backdrop that the history of the voiceless although a very popular type of history has not gained much currency in Cameroon historiography. In other parts of the continent and beyond this type of history has already been at its infancy. Yet the Cameroonian example shows that it is at its embryonic stage. This might generally be because this type of historical narratives has not appealed to scholars working on Cameroon. Cameroon history has been replete with studies that focuses mostly on political history and which mostly deal with the top politicians of the day (Ngoh, 1985 and 2001; Johnson, 1970; Levine, 1971; Fanso, 1988; Krieger and Takougang, 1995; Krieger, 2008; Rubin, 1971)

In this introductory chapter, I intend to give the voiceless a thought as it has been presented by some scholars in the literature. After that I will expand the horizons of the characteristic features of such a notion and then see how I intend to explore it in this volume. The second section examines some methodological aspects and sources which were used to arrive at this book. The third section will offer a synopsis of the various arteries that make up the body of the book also adding the new material that has been uncovered in due course from the archives, oral interviews and secondary materials.

## Towards Understanding Voiceless Voices

The notion of voiceless has been receiving a lively debate for sometime now in the academia. Simply put it refers to those set of people who have contributed towards the production of history but who have not received a commensurate reward in the historical research and writings because it is largely accepted that the people are from the lower rungs of the society. The type of history that has been produced here is the history of the people without the voices so to say as opposed to people with voices who hold the reins of power and were at the centre of power. This has been widely held in the academia as the subalterns. While not very anxious to embark on the nuances of that terminology it will as well be crucial for the reader to have a gist of what constitutes the subalterns both in the extant literature and how it can fit into the frame of this current debate.

According to the Oxford English Dictionary the term subaltern has three meanings: it is conventionally understood as a synonym of subordinate, but it can also denote a lower ranking officer in the army, or a particular example that supports a universal proposition in philosophical logic. Historiographically, the term is traced to Spivak who in her authoritative work, "Can the Subalterns Speak" (1988:271-313) appeared to have opened the floodgates for scholars to embark on such studies but the term appeared to have been in usage even before 1988. In that essay the author's question develops a post colonial theory, which interrogates how subaltern gendered subjectivity was framed in the context of British imperialism's intervention into the practice of *sati* (window immolation) in India. According to one of his disciples, Morton (2007:95-96), Spivak's work centered on the role of the radical western intellectual rather than the subaltern historian as a spokesperson or proxy for the oppressed or disempowered groups. Morton continued and maintained that Spivak gained inspiration from the Italian Marxist, Antonio Gramsci on the rural based Italian peasantry and the research of the international Subaltern Studies collective on the histories of subaltern insurgency in colonial and post colonial South Asia (For more see, Williams, 2002 and Guya *et. al.*,2002; Partha, 2006; Eva, 1996; Priyamvada, 2004, Antonio, 2003;Ranagit and Spivak, 1989;Ranajit, 1989; Sarkar, 1997;Rodriguez, 2005 and 2001; Ravel and Hunt,1995; Verdesio, 2005; Williams 2006; Chaturvedi, 2000; Guha and Spivak, 1989; Scott, 1990 and 1985;Ergene, 1998;Mallon, 1994).

In this book I have critically engaged in the argument of the above scholars and at the same time see the subaltern without much limitation. I have tried as much as possible to minimize essentialist views of looking at the notion through analogy rather than through context. This means that my use of the voiceless even includes those in the corridors of power who more often are neglected in the subaltern discourses. By doing so this discourse becomes more flexible and interesting.

One dominant school of subaltern history is held naturally to have emerged from Asia and more from India. Those subaltern studies have changed the intellectual landscapes in South Asian studies and beyond. Researchers who belonged to that school have focused attention on the social relations of rural society-relations of domination and control, relations of un-freedom, relations of power and authority between landlord and tenant, master and bondsman. They have influenced me with limitations no doubt to see the ways in which South Asian studies emerged within the conceptual categories of British colonial administration.

From the readings, I can understand that these trajectories which has emerged from the above school is very specific due to its ethnic histories, its patterns of landholding and labour, its pre-colonial and colonial history. Secondly, "the category of subaltern is an intuitively attractive point of departure for South Asianists, given the widely shared perception of social distinction in India as long lasting, coercive, and sharply delineated....(Cooper,1994:1519). But then I could also understand from my readings that South East Asian history is also much more complex because of its agrarian civilization which wove up the social phenomena with very strong resonances to other parts of the world. Other areas of the world has also developed dynamic traditions of agrarian histories so to say and historical research is oriented towards the saga and environments of the powerless, research that questions traditional categories of politics and the empire, research that cast strong light on the darkness of peasant resistance and rebellion (see Gail, 1986; Aston and Philipin, 1985; Lucien, 1986; Kang, 1986; Hoeber, 1987:731-746; O,Hanlon, 1988; Vlastos, 1986). The kernel of the question which comes to the fore now is whether there is the possibility of a fruitful exchange between the subaltern approach to South Asian studies and current research in other agrarian or semi-agrarian societies?

In African historiography, the impact of Subaltern Studies has not been felt very strongly in the continent. Scholars have increasingly mentioned Subaltern Studies but a bulk of such studies which have taken centre-stage on Subaltern Studies comes from South Africa (Moore, 1998: 344-381;Mitchell, 2002: 431-450; Lalu, 1998: 133-159; Cooper, 1994 and 2004). These scholars have not yet come to a consensus with the concept of subaltern autonomy because it is believed that in South Africa boundary lines between race and class are clearly and sharply defined. Bahl (2000) shows that another difference between Indian Subalternists and African historians is that Indian scholars have been trying to dismantle the idea of an essential "India" by insisting on differences within communities and identities. Bahl (2002) went further and said:

> Moreover, Africanists do not find the subalternists ideas new or earthshaking. For example, Subaltern Studies focuses mainly on the problems of recovering histories while understanding how colonial documents construct their own colonialist versions of those histories. This methodology appears to the African historians to be sound practice than a methodological breakthrough. In the 1960s, African historians learned that colonial sources distorted history; they found a solution by using oral sources as well as reading colonial documents against the grain. In addition, in the process of writing a people's history, African scholars place more emphasis on showing that Africans had a history than on asking how the African's history-making is implicated in establishing or contesting power.

This sounds a defense on the part of African historians for not taking up Subaltern Studies with the seriousness it deserved. I find that excuse quite intriguing and could only have a strong base as far as the number of works on the continent as compared to that elsewhere in Asia and India is concern. Yet there has been some break thorough works out of South Africa on Subalterns although the authors never directly mentioned that they were dealing with subaltern. For instance, thirty years before, Subaltern was coined; Kenneth Onwuka Dike defended his PhD thesis, *Trade and Politics in the Niger Delta* (1956). Dike attempted with much success to write history from an African perspective. In his thesis, he presented the Africans as neither resisters nor collaborators in the face of European involvement. Kandeh (2004) examines the subalterns from the military dimension. In (1999: 349-366) he also documented the place of elites' origins of the Subalterns terror in Sierra Leone. "He situates the transformation of praetorian violence from a tool of political domination to a means of criminal expropriation in the engendering context of elite parasitism and repression". Iliffe (1987 and Feierman, 1990; Ranger, 1983 and 1985), essentially wrote the history of the subalterns although not admittedly explicit. Iliffe for instance, in *the African Poor: a history* writes the history of the subaltern. He admits in the first page (p.1) that "the old imperial history was marred by an elitism which because the elite were often a tiny minority white, could degenerate further into radicalism. The national histories that have replaced it, by contrast, are marred by their parochialism. To escape both defects requires a ... social history which treats people...."

These snapshots however could safe as indicators and points to a signboard-that subaltern studies had started in Africa although not much had been covered in that domain. This volume is a contribution towards the growth of such studies from an African perspective and with focus on Cameroon.

The subalterns as used here go beyond the original way that was meant to be used in the 1980s but yet not totally breaking with the linearity of the term itself. The chapters here are not in a *stricto senso* diverting from the way the subalterns have been handled elsewhere.

Yet I must state upfront to the benefit of the reader that my usage of the term is quite elastic and flexible. For instance it will bother the reader to know how I want to use the elites. Elites generally has been used in the literature as first amongst equals-primus inter pares as seen by Italian sociologists, Mosca and Pareto. Although they are largely seen through such binoculars the Cameroonian example seemed to show the extra-ordinary. The elites manipulate what I will call the masses and the elites themselves are also manipulated by those who think they are the vote holders of the state. The state in turn is manipulated by the metropolitan power-France. So at the end of the day we have what I have coined here as "ever diminishing circles of subalternity". Subalterns remain ubiquitous and it only depends how and with which eye we look at them and in what situation. The seven chapters are therefore out to add something to the existing body of literature with special focus on Cameroon history and again a new type of history in Cameroon which might yield dividends to those who would be interested in carrying out future research.

5

By doing so, I draw my inspiration from three scholars. The first of these scholars is Allain Touraine whose concept of historicity is the ability of the community to provide an orientation and transform itself in the process and more relevant to me is his model of talking about a people's history. Another scholar was Harneiet Sievers (2002) and his colleagues. According to him a history of the voiceless is an attempt to write the history from the perspective of people below the level of official positions. It also includes history from the official statements and announcements made from the political platforms. I will like to point out here that the word voiceless as used in this context does not refer to a particular status of people. What is important is that their voices need to be heard in as much as they were recorded. In a way the voices of the voiceless which was not heard need to be heard in Cameroon history. I have not yet come across a volume which discusses the history of the voiceless in Cameroon. So I have in this volume woven various themes with diverse backgrounds which hitherto have not been known in Cameroon historiography.

The new vista which I wish to open in this book will follow the reasoning of Ludden (2001) and to a lesser extent, Mallon, (1994). The two scholars have attempted with much success to analyse and interpret the waning of subaltern studies and have shown by far the multifaceted sides that underlie the meanings as posited by the term subaltern. For instance and I quote, Ludden(2001:8) has demonstrated that:

> Subaltern Studies does not mean today what it meant in 1982, 1983 and 1985. How did this change occur? Intellectual environments have changed too much to allow us measure cause-and-effect in particular acts of writing and reading. Change has occurred inside the Subaltern Studies project, but ambiguously, as will see, and how much internal change is cause or effect of external change is unknowable, because inside and outside, subaltern subjects have been reinvented desperately. When approaching the intellectual history of subalternity, it will not do to imagine that Subaltern Studies dropped a weighty stone into a quiet pond, or to trace the influence of teachers and students, or to speculate that cutting-edge ideas have dispersed globally like news on the internet…a

compact but complex history of reading and writing has constituted the subject of subalternity in a widening world of scholarship, where some readers accept and others reject the claim that Subaltern Studies represents the real substance of subalternity, even in India. The intellectual history of subalternity has emerged outside and in opposition to Subaltern Studies as much as inside it. Academic work on subaltern themes quickly detached subalternity from its various inventors.

People live in a dynamic and changing world so do their thinking and actions. Ludden has shown from the above that the usage of the term subaltern no matter what it meant to its founders has changed in recent times therefore it does not make sense if we continue to think about it in purely essentialist terms. Writing on civil society in 2009, Konings showed that civil society needs to be used within context rather than just lifting it up from one end of the globe and then impose it on another. Konings (2009:1) maintains unequivocally that, "a concept that is borrowed from Western discourse needs to be contextualized in a comparative manner to adequately capture and explain the African reality".

**A brief note on sources and methods**
Methodologically, the material that has become the result of what I have here is as a result of research work which provisionally started in the Buea National Archives when I first entered there in October 1993 just two months at my undergraduate program in the University. My continuous search for the truth, the subject of all science, took me to various libraries and archives around the globe. I visited the Public Records Archive, Kew Gardens, London in November 2007; Mission 21 archives at missionstraase, Basel in 2008; The Afrika-Studie Centrum library, Leiden, The Netherlands periodically from September to December 2007 and from September 2009 to March 2010. I also participated at international workshops like the workshop on Governing Elites in Africa which took place in Dakar, Senegal from August to September 2003 and the other one Historicizing migrations which coincidentally took place in Dakar but this time at Saint Louis just to name a few. In these workshops

my views on several notions were sharpened and I came to look at things differently. Through intellectual pollination with other senior scholars my historical back was straightened. I also extensively used oral tradition and /or oral testimonies. The importance of oral tradition, in societies whose written word has not been at centre stage cannot be neglected. When I talked about marginalised I mean pre-literate societies in the western sense and which writing too in the western sense has not been the order of the day. These are societies which never had western forms of writing from the beginning. The information which will be produced by way of mouth will try to fill the gaps of what was presented in the archives to an extent. In the introduction to the *General History of Africa* the celebrated African historian from Burkina Faso, Joseph Ki-Zerbo (1990:7) said:

> Oral tradition takes its place as a real living museum, conserver and transmitter of the social and cultural creations stored up by peoples said to have no written records....Oral tradition is by far the most intimate of historical sources, the most rich, the one which is fullest of the sap of authenticity....However useful the written record, it is bound to freeze, to dry up its subject. It decants, dissects, schematizes, and petrifies: the letter killeth. Tradition clothes things in the flesh and blood and colour, it gives blood to the skeleton of the past. It presents in three dimensions what is often crowded on to the two dimensional surface of a piece of paper.

Although Ki-Zerbo poured so many encomiums on oral tradition it is worth noting that it has its own drawbacks which he did not hesitate to outline them. According to him, "this spoken history is a very frail thread by which we use to trace our way back through the dark twists of the labyrinth of time". He continued by saying that "Those who are its custodians are hoary-headed old men with cracked voices, memories often dim, and a stickler's insistence on etiquette as behoves potential ancestors". He ended up by saying that: "They are like the last remaining islets in a landscape that was once imposing and coherent, but which is now eroded, flattened and thrown into disorder by the sharp waves of modernity". Jan Vansina (1985:199) and Miller(1980), often quoted as the doyen of African oral tradition complemented in the conclusion of his authoritative work, opining that "oral traditions have a part to play in the reconstruction of the past. The importance of this part varies according to place and time. It is a part similar to that played by written sources because both are messages from the past to the present, and messages are key elements in historical reconstruction". Writing very recently, Maiga(2010:2), upheld the place of oral history in Africa by showing that it will be difficult, for the reconstruction of any history *let alone Cameroon history* without oral testimonies.

Whatever the case, the importance of oral tradition borne out through interview was rigorously handled during the research to produce what is found here. Even though oral tradition might suffer some shortcomings as well as the written sources, a combination of the two might yield better evidence than one. Ryder (1970:33) was aware of this shortcoming. He remarked that "Too often it is assumed that anything written must be more reliable than verbal testimony; but every historian knows that a written document needs to be subjected to exactly the same sort of scrutiny as to the circumstances in which it was produced as does a piece of oral evidence. The word of mouth is no more or less subject to distortion, deliberate or accidental, than the written word". The subjectivity of both sources does not in any sense means that their importance should be negated. Their importance could be gotten by the combination of the two. This is because either the archival or the oral are defective in one way or another. To take full advantage of the results it is therefore central for us to get the two sources.

Oral tradition per se was very important to the finalization of this book. Rangers (2000), advises a historian of Africa with an example of the kind of research that has to be done in Africa. He advises that in writing the history of the African continent it is important to use the sources found there as much as possible like oral tradition and I think I have used enough oral testimonies in this book. With this in mind I have always found it imperative to use as many sources as possible but at the same time feels that more sources especially on archives during the colonial period are more in Europe than in Africa. I also tried to consult them. In very rare situations I used photographs which were really fascinating. Photographs capture the reality and could be very compelling to the reader (Roberts, 1988).

**Structure of the Book**

The volume consists of eight chapters that are based on articles which I have written in the first half of the $21^{st}$ Century (2003-2009). These essays captures in one way or another on the various themes in Cameroon history which according to me much attention has not been paid with focus on what the scholars felt that it was negligible. Secondly, the chapters have received attention from academics in different perspectives and time and space. I consulted many scholarly works on various topics. This burgeon literature although not an exhaustive one is suggestive of the various topics which I have brought together here. It therefore announces that the chapters here have been variously handled in the literature. But what is lacking according to me is that I have not yet come across any single volume that handles issues as diverse as the ones I have coalesced in this volume.

As I earlier indicated there are no doubts a few chapters that will stray off the main thread of the argument like the ones on football, elites and civil society which actually falls in the post colonial period of Cameroon history. They none the less still have a bearing on the main thread of the book. In some of the chapters I have added new and fresh information which I tumbled over in the course of doing research since the articles were published. The first chapter is the introduction in which I introduce the book to the reader in a short precise way.

Chapter two analyses the first serious female revolution which erupted towards the end of the British colonial rule in the British Southern Cameroon. That revolution occurred in the Kom Fondom, the second largest Fondom in the Bamenda grassfields. That episode has attracted so far a good number of researchers and scholars who did some brilliant work although some weaknesses remained glaring over the years. The first weakness lies in the fact that although almost all the researchers have spoken about the Agricultural law which precipitated the revolution, no researcher has actually given the full text of the law. What was it? How was it formulated? I have attempted to quote that law here. The second weakness is that most of the writers have spoken about Jua who was behind the *anlu* but it has not been found anywhere in the literature that the wife of Jua played any role. Where was she during the political turbulence of that women revolution?

Thirdly, Muana and Fuam have been repeatedly handled in the literature I have added to their role their photograph which they took with the politicians of their day like Jua, Foncha and some traditional rulers. Finally the march of the women to Bamenda and the constant visits of the British administrators to Njinikom called to question who their translator was. This question led to me to discover their translator who was also a woman amongst those who were on strike. I have also included her role. These and several issues like the symbols which they employed have also been added in chapter one.

Another weaknesses which I suffered in the first paper which I published and which I still think was a very grave error was to examine the Kom women revolution in the ongoing global literature of women's rebellions especially in Africa. Which theories informed the revolution and what was the meaning of exposing the bodies and vulgar parts of the body. The universality of the wrangle over women contribution to historical phenomena has brought to the limelight several contending but relevant postulations. Early advocates of theories like De Beauvoir (1952) argue that women play second fiddle to men as the second sex. The reason advanced is that women are constrained to reproducing and sustaining life and nothing more. This contention known as cultural dualism emphasises the dual action of men celebrating but also denigrating women. Another theorist who wrote a pioneering work on women and development in developing areas is Ester Boserup. An exponent of the social evolutionary school, Boserup (1970) argues that women are often relegated to the backward sector of the economy and deprived of participating in community wide decisions. Going by this social evolutionary theory, women do not really influence the life of a society.

For the sustainers of the dependency school like Martha Mueller (1977), the urban and landed elite create opportunities for men in towns and cause them to abandon women to community life back home. Besides, exponents of the developmentalist school like Inkeles and Smith (1974) point to separate development opportunities for men and women. They also argue that when women happen to be employed, their employers who are mostly men exploit them. There are contemporary theories outlined in March *et al* (1999). These theories highlight four frames of analysis on gender among which are the Harvard Analytical framework, the People-Oriented Planning framework, Moser and the Women Empowerment or Longwe frameworks. These frameworks notwithstanding, the early theories of De Beauvoir and Boserup are still relevant to the experience the Kom women had during the colonial era. They were relegated to the background by men due to the nature of the British colonial policy.

Other scholars have examined the different meanings attached to the body, symbolism, sexuality and bodily practices of different people the world over. According to Connerton (1989:74) much of the choreography of authority is expressed through the body in all cultures. Smith on the other hand (1997:184-6) drawing his conclusions from a study of the Kuba, Turkana, Igbo and Frafra of the Democratic Republic of the Congo, Kenya, Nigeria and Ghana respectively generally describes the issue of dress on the body in the light of a people with shared views and experience on a complex set of items. In these societies there is a contextual way of analysing issues that relate to the body. In his own view, Roberts (1997:192) describes symbolism as a process that evolves and meaning changes with time. He posits that symbols are used to express a people's dynamic worldview. These are indeed the basis of any ritual religious, political or economic understanding which is however always subjected to debate.

Besides, issues of symbols and meanings have also been examined by Davis, Bordo, Frank and Crawford. Davis (1997:2) argues and is supported by Bordo (1993) and Crawford (1984:80) that bodies are used for self expression. This makes people to become who they would like to be. According to Davis (1997:7) and Bordo (1993) the female body is the object of processes of domination and control. It is also the site of women's subversive practices and struggles for self determination and empowerment. On his part, Frank (1990:133) contends that the body is the 'only constant in a rapidly changing world and has remained the source of fundamental truths about who people are and how society is organised. It is true that the body has been subjected to different descriptions and interpretations by different people and societies but they always share similar and dissimilar concerns.

12

With regards to the Kom of Cameroon, women used their bodies and other bodily gesticulations and symbols to protest against domination in the closing years of British colonial rule. The aim was empowerment in economic and political matters under the colonial dispensation. They realised that their aim would be frustrated if they did not resort to certain 'deadly' bodily practices to frighten the men and the colonial administration into submission. The colonial environment had projected the Kom men into prominence through new economic, political and social structures. The women mass uprising and use of bodily gesticulations petrified the traditional and colonial authorities. These are issues which I felt were very relevant to add to this study which six years ago I could not add to this research.

Chapter three is more or less the continuation of chapter one in another dimension. That dimension situates the place of ingenuity of the African in his/ her creativity around his environment. This is more captivating in the songs which were produced in Kom, although I have illustrated enough from songs which were created from other areas in Africa. In the treatment given to the songs I have tried as much as possible with resounding success to recover the history and agency of the subaltern. I have also gone further to examine the songs as alternative sources for historical construction of the Kom people. Which type of history can be read from songs? This is not new in African history because it has been handled elsewhere in Africa. Unfortunately, Cameroon history has not benefited much from such a repertoire. I have added new information to that chapter on the song that was about the TRAPP. That information is to dispel the fact which was dearly held in most quarters in Kom that the Cameroon government did not have anything to do with the construction of the road which was constructed between 1993 and 1996.

Chapter four describes one of the most significant events which have haunted the African continent in general and the Bamenda Grassfields of Cameroon in particular. This has been the boundary conflicts. This chapter instead of taking all the boundary conflicts in that sub region has decided to take the Bambili/Babanki Tungoh from C. 1955 to 1998. The chapter begins by looking at the framework of colonial boundaries in Africa and then narrows down

**13**

to the causes, course and consequences of the boundary conflict. It ends by providing solutions that if well implemented will no doubt bring an end to the boundary misunderstanding in the region and beyond. The chapter has added fresh material from the Buea National archives by using files which numbered well over twenty-five. Those files also gave a broadened panorama of the various disputes which had occurred in the grassfields. They included: File Qf/a (1) 1933, Intertribal boundaries settlement ordinance, Buea; File Qf/b (2) 1943, Bali-Bamengen land disputes, Bamenda Division; File Qf/f(1) 1950. Mukuru-Nkoromanjang land disputes: Boundary dispute, Babadji village versus Okoromanjang; File Qf/b(1) 1936, Bambunji-Babujang village groups, Bamenda Division, Boundary dispute; File Qf/b(2) 1939, Bangangu-Bambetu land dispute, Bamenda Division; File Qf/b (1) 1938, Bande- Bangwa boundary dispute, Bamenda Division and a host of other file as well were used.

Chapter five diverts into a domain which has taken centre-stage in intellectual debate amongst the academia since the 1990s both in Cameroon and beyond-the politics of belonging. In this chapter I generally take the debate from a global dimension and situate a case study in Cameroon which is the South West Elites Association also known by its acronym, SWELA. That association was formed in 1991 and it disintegrated into its component parts in 1997. In that chapter I examined the antecedents of that association and treat the association within the category of elite literature.

Chapter six examines another aspect of Cameroon history that has remained mired in the archives so far but which was nonetheless very instrumental for the success of the daily *horarium* of the colonial project. These were the telephone operators whom the British colonial managers treated as though they were objects. This category of people although very important to the greasing of the colonial machinery has remained silent in the Cameroon historiographical discourses.

Chapter seven takes a look at the civil society in Cameroon. My intension here is to revisit it in the current debates in Cameroon and proffer some suggestions. The final chapter looks at football and the politics of belonging both at the internal level and also at the international levels as well. It demonstrates how football has been romancing with the politics in Cameroon. Each of these chapters begins with a short introduction and ends with a short conclusion.

# Chapter Two

## The *Anlu* Factor and the 1959 Elections in the British Southern Cameroons: The Case of Kom Fondom, 1958-1961

### Introduction

This chapter has the following goals: firstly, it sets out to investigate why and how the *Anlu* influenced the outcome of the 1959 elections in the Kom fondom of the British Southern Cameroons. Secondly, it attempts to show how the Kamerun National Democratic Party (KNDP) in the Kom fondom was shrewd to use *the Anlu* to achieve its political goals. 'Primary and secondary sources were consulted during the research and from them, it is evident that the *Anlu* campaigned and convinced the electorate to vote in favour of the KNDP. Furthermore, the KNDP politicians were astute enough to manipulate the *Anlu* to gain votes in the 1959 elections and as a result contributed in influencing the destiny of British Southern Cameroons. Beyond these goals the chapter explores the use of symbols which the *Anlu* women. Who was the translator of these women when the colonial administrators came visiting them or when they march to Bamenda?

**The *Anlu*** was a traditional society that existed before 1958 in the Kom Fondom of the Southern Cameroons. At its inception, it was aimed at redressing grievances committed against women by men as well as husbands against their wives. In 1958, it took a political dimension following the application of an agricultural law by the ruling Kamerun National Congress party (KNC) which was misunderstood by the *Anlu* and its members who subsequently revolted against it in 1958. As a result of the revolt, *Anlu* became active in the politics of the Kom fondom in particular and the Bamenda grassfields in general. During its political activities, the Kamerun National Democratic Party (KNDP) apparently used it for political gains. Soon after the 1959 elections, the political activities of *Anlu* decreased and by 1961 the, *Anlu* had petered out as a political force.

Several scholars have written on this topic[1] but they have done so either from a sociological, anthropological or missionary point of view. Those who have written from the political and/or historical point of view have not, in the opinion of this writer, given enough emphasis on how the *Anlu* influenced the outcome of the 1959 elections in the Kom fondom. (see Ritzenthaler,1960; Nkwain, 1958 and 1963; Chilver and Kaberry, 1975; Nkwi,1976; Rogers,1980; O'Barr,1984; Nkwi, 1985; Diduk, 1989; Konde, 1990; Shanklin,1990; O'Neil, 1991; Westernman, 1992; Malcom, 1999).

## Kom in Geographical and ethnographic terms

The Fondom of Kom which is the axle of this study is located in the Bamenda Grassfields of Cameroon. The Bamenda Grassfields as I used it in this study refers to the present day Northwest Region of Cameroon. Its ecology of almost grasslands as opposed to the forest region of Cameroon made the Germans to name the place the Bamenda Grasslands. The politics in the grasslands are dominated or organized around the Fondoms or chiefdoms which are ruled by Fons. These Fondoms, in general grew out of an aggressive politics; politics of inclusion and exclusion through warfare which led to the subjugation of weaker neighbours. They were characterized by clear political and social hierarchies related to kinship relations or lineages, social and political status. Most studies have focused on the chiefdoms and on the creation of political hegemony and social organizations, (see Chilver and Kaberry, 1967; Nkwi, 1976; Warnier, 2007; Argenti, 2007 and Rowlands, 1979).

Kom is variedly spelt in colonial and some post colonial records as Bikom, Bekom Bamungkom and Nkom but for the purpose of this study, Kom will be adapted. It is the second largest Fondom after Nso in the Bamenda Grassfields of Cameroon. It shares its eastern boundary with the kingdoms of Oku and Nso and the southern frontier with Kedjom Keku (Big Babanki) and Ndop plain. Bafut occupies the Western border while to the north is found Bum and Mmen. Nkwi (1976) has given a detail study of the ethnography and geography of Kom. In terms of development Kom and the other parts of the Bamenda Grassfields has not benefited much from the development projects of the Cameroon government. It has thus remained at the fringes of the state development in what anthropologists like Das and Poole (1991) calls "the margins of the state". By that phrase they simply refer to areas which are often depicted as being marginal/subordinate, and that marginality is in a way related to geography, economy, social and politics. The people of those areas also see themselves as marginal in relationship to the state. The state therefore constitute the dominant others. The contradiction in terms of those marginal areas is that although the crest "marginal" might sometimes suggest "cut off", the people who dwell in those areas have on the other hand always been part and geographical mobility links them to the centre of affairs although in a timid way. The Kom Fondom is just an example of such areas that make up the Bamenda Grassfields.

The Kom Fondom as used here was founded around the middle of the 19th Century. It also includes the congeries of sub chiefdoms which were incorporated into Kom proper as "vassal states" by Fon Yu, the seventh ruler of Kom. These tributary chiefdoms included: Achain, Ake, Ajung, Mbesinaku, Mbueni, Baiso, Baicham, Mejang, Mbengkas and Mejung. According to the Kom oral traditions, their ancestors migrated from Ndobo in North Cameroon with other Tikar groups to Babessi where they settled temporarily (For more on Tikar with its controversies see (Evans, 1926 Ch). A popular legend recounts their movement from Babessi to their present settlement. It states that while the Kom people were at Babessi, their population increased tremendously that it frightened the King of Babessi who devised a trick to eliminate the kom people. One day the king of Babessi told the Fon of Kom that some of their people were becoming obstinate and might cause a war between their two groups and thus proposed that they should each build a house in which the trouble makers would be burnt. The Fon of Kom, Muni, agreed to the plan and the houses were constructed accordingly but while the king of Babessi constructed his house with two doors, the guiltless Muni built his own house according to instructions, with only one door. After locking the front doors, the houses were set ablaze. The Babessi people escaped through the second door while the Kom people were burnt to death. This trick that reduced Kom population in Babessi made the Fon very angry.

The oral tradition further informed me that because of the anger and frustrations Muni promised to his remnant wives and sisters that he would revenge the death of his people. He told them that

**17**

he would hung himself on a tree in a nearby forest and on that spot a lake will developed and all the maggots that will come out from his decomposing body will turn into fish in that lake. The lake was discovered by a Babessi hunter and immediately reported to the palace. A royal fishing was organised. At the peak of the fishing the lake "somersaulted" and all the Babessi people who were in the lake drowned. Following Muni's instructions the tract of a python, believed to be the incarnated Fon led the Kom people from Babessi to Nkar and Idien (Djottin) in the present day Bui Division of Northwest Cameroon. At Idien they settled near a stream beside a raffia bush. There, the Queen mother, Tih, brought forth a son who was to be the next king. That son was called Jingjua meaning suffering near a stream. She also gave birth to Nange Tih, future mother of the *Ikui* clan, Nakhinti Tih, future mother of *Itinalah* and Ndzitewa Tih, future mother of the *Achaff* clan. Once the python trail reappeared the Kom left Idien for Ajung where the python's trail disappeared again. At Ajung the Fon of Ajung got married to Nangeh Tih and brought forth Jinabo, Nangebo, Nyanga and Bi. After a while the Python's tract reappeared and the Kom left again for Laikom. From there the ancestors of two clans in Kom-*Ndotitichia* and *Ijinasung* joined the trekkers through the Ijim forest to Laikom where the python disappeared (more about Kom has been discussed in chapter three)

The Fon is the paramount ruler of a fondom and is usually associated with divine powers and quasi-religious functions. The Kom Fondom is one of the largest in the Northwest Cameroon, popularly known in colonial historiography as the Bamenda Grassfields. It shares its eastern boundary with the kingdoms of Oku and Nso and the Southern frontier with the Kidjem Kelu (Big Babanki) and Ndop plains. Bafut occupies the Western border, while to the North is found Bum and Mmen (Kiawi, 2001:1-8). Before 1993, Kom was under Menchum Division from which Boyo Division was created. Kom contains three of the Sub Divisions that make up Belo, Njinikom and Fundong. It shares boundaries with four of the seven divisions of the Northwest Provinces - Mezam, Menchum, Ngoketunjia and Bui divisions. The present boundary of Kom owe to the expansionist policies of Fon Yuh (Chilver and Kaberry, 1967).

## *Anlu* is Born

According to Kom oral and written literature, there are conflicting views with regard to the origin of *Anlu*. One school of thought, led by Veronica Bongbi, maintains that when the Kom journeyed from Babessi to Laikom, they were constantly harassed by their neighbours - Mejang, Ajung, Bafmeng and Kijem. Kom subsequently became a vassal state under Ajung and Mejang which meant that she had to pay tribute to Ajung and Mejang. The Kom were required, amongst others, to perform difficult tasks for their masters. For instance, the Kom were required to use castor oil instead of water to mix mud that was used for the construction of houses in the Mejang palace.

At one stage, the Kom people refused to perform this duty and this was considered by the Mejang as an act of rebellion which had to be suppressed. The opportune moment came when the Fon of Kom and his men went to pay tribute to Ajung. The Mejang warriors invaded Laikom, capital of the Kom fondom, with the intention of taking the women and children as prisoners of war. By doing so, it was expected that the Kom would be brought back under the control of Mejang. Unfortunately for the Mejang warriors, the Kom women bravely resisted the invasion under the instructions of their Queen Mother, *Nafoyn*. She asked the women to dress themselves in men's clothes and take their weapons. The Mejang warriors mistook them for men and fled. It is said that during the struggle, many Mejang warriors died while some escaped. Only a physically deformed man was captured by the Kom women. The Kom women stripped themselves off their war garments to reveal their true identity to the captured Mejang warrior. The deformed man was astonished. He was instructed to tell the chief and the people of Mejang that they were to pay tribute from thence to Kom. This, it is said, saw the beginning *of Anlu*. (Nkwi, 1985:185) Nkwi shares the same view with Bongbi and Mumukom and I think this version is authentic.

Another school of thought led by Francis I. Nkwain maintains that *Anlu* came into existence when:

> Owing to trickery by an enemy, all the active male members of the [Kom] community were once slaughtered. To defend the group the women declared themselves in vines. The women kept guard and repelled enemy attacks while the few old men built the houses, hunted for food, went and paid the required tributes to Ajung. (Nkwain, 1963).

**19**

Nkwain was the first Kom man to document anything on *Anlu*. In this article Nkwain accepts the fact that the *1958 Anlu* was politically instigated yet he fails to show how this was done as well as how this influenced the outcome of the 1959 elections in the Kom fondom.

This account seems to suggest that the origins *of Anlu* took place at Babessi. This is because owing to a trick, almost half of the active male population was destroyed. Secondly, to say that after the "genocide" women declared themselves in vines and kept guard at Babessi is simply without foundation in Kom oral and written literature (For more on the Kom migratory history see Chilver and Kaberry, 1967: 123-151; Evans, 1927; Jeffrey, 1952:200-215; Ngoh, 1996: 9-10)

On the strength of the above, I think that this version vis-à-vis the origin of *Anlu* (Shanklin, 1990:160) should not be taken seriously and *ipso facto,* should be dismissed. The *Anlu* in its traditional setting was meant to protect women's rights and in a sense maintain social equilibrium in the fondom. These rights included *inter alia:* beating a pregnant woman or a nursing mother by the husband, maltreatment of one's mother or father, insulting the womanhood of a woman, and committing incest or any crime that dehumanised the woman. (Personal communication with Ambrose Beng, Njinikom, 16 August 1999).From the above objectives, it is evident that *Anlu* before 1958 was out to redress grievances committed against women by men and vice versa and it was neatly organised to carry out its functions.

**Organisation and Activities**

Initiated on a military basis, *Anlu* was organised along the lines of *Njong,* a village military club. The leader of *Anlu* was called *Na-anlu* (the mother of *Anlu)* who was usually the oldest woman in the village. When the women enforced an effective ban on a person, *Na-anlu* coordinated all actions taken against the individual concerned. She was assisted by spies *(ugwesii)* who were led by the *na-gwesii* (mother of spies). These spies were chosen from privileged families and their main task was to see that the culprit was isolated from the rest of the community and punish those who sought social contact with the guilty person. Most of the written literature has failed to acknowledge the fact that these spies were chosen from particular families. These families were families that had a royal leaning and were noted as the families which were the founders of Kom Fondom.

The organisation, as at 1958, was slightly different. The queen was at the pinnacle of the organisational chart and determined the policy. Next to her was the spokesperson who was popularly known as the "Divisional Officer". She was responsible for the making of announcements. There were the "neighbourhood heads" and spies who met with the queen from time to time and took instructions; next there were the messengers whose responsibilities were to summon the people for interviews or meetings, the scribes or sanitary officers who pretended to record rules which have been passed in the meeting and finally there were the jesters, whose functions were to entertain the crowd at large meetings (See Ritzenthaler, 1961: 153)

This organisation was to facilitate the activities *of Anlu* yet the usage of "D.O.", "Scribes" or "Sanitary officer" seemed to have a deeper meaning. Since the final outbreak of *Anlu* was against the KNC as a party and Bartholomew Chia Kiyam as an individual, the adoption of such a nomenclature was derogatory. It was also aimed at ridiculing the Western method of administration. That notwithstanding, the organisation *of Anlu* in 1958 touched on all the nooks and crannies of the Kom fondom and beyond. According to Nkwain in his 1963 mimeograph, the *Anlu* mechanism was set into motion when a woman doubled into a grotesque posture and uttered a shrill high-pitched sound which was interrupted at intervals by smacking four fingers on the lips; this was the signal for action." First of all, the members abandoned whatever they were doing and moved off in the direction of the initial sound, imitating it as they moved along. As the members assembled, they performed a dance accompanied by impromptu verse through which the offence committed was spelt out in such a manner as to create emotional response.

A whispering session ensued during which the offence was recounted. The women then invoked the offender's ancestors for the necessary support after which they would go to the bush from where they would only return on an appointed time, usually just

**21**

before dawn, donned in vines, pieces of men's clothing and painted faces for the full ritual. They carried a garden-egg type fruit which supposedly caused all those who were knocked with it to "dry up". Later the members *of Anlu* would assemble at the offender's compound singing, dancing, defecating and urinating at every turn. In the course of all this, they would behave like savages exhibiting even the most intimate parts of their bodies (vaginas) and singing weird song (Nkwain, 1963: 5).

From the above description, there is need for attention to be drawn on some key issues with regard to the activities of the *Anlu*. Firstly, only women were involved and no man or any of the traditional judicial institution could step in. During this period, the social and political affairs of the village were entirely in the hands of the women and they could virtually force their husbands to carry out domestic chores. Secondly, some gestures seemed to indicate the reversal of the natural order of things. According to the Kom mind, it was abnormal for women to put on dresses that were meant for men. It is equally unacceptable for parts of the body like the vagina to be exposed. Culturally, a lot of importance is attach to vaginas in Kom because it is assumed that vagina is the entire "womanhood" of a woman and should be treated with decency and decorum.

Furthermore, it was not normal for a woman to neither paint herself with wood ash nor use another person's compound as a public toilet. It was even more absurd to stone a person with a garden egg-like fruit *(funya)* because it symbolized the drying of the individual. All these actions, considered to be outside the normal order of things, were performed by the *Anlu* to show the gravity of the offence committed. In its totality, the activities of *Anlu* showed awkwardness and absurdity in the widest form. The activities of *Anlu* were later politicised in the Kom fondom in particular and the Bamenda grassfields in general in the late 1950s.

## Party Politics in the Kom Fondom

There were three political parties in Kom by the late 1950s: the KNC, the Kamerun Peoples Party (KPP) and the KNDP. The KPP was never active in Kom, partly because it lacked leadership as well as membership and partly because between 1956 and 1961, it had a similar political platform with the KNC. However, the first indigenous party to be formed in the Southern Cameroons was the KNC. From its inception, the party had as its ideology, the separation of British Southern Cameroons from Nigeria. It was because of this and several other reasons that the party registered successes in the 1954 elections. Despite this, its leader, Dr. E.M.L. Endeley, and some KNC members began talking more and more in terms of autonomy within Nigeria. With the various shades of opinion within the KNC, KNC members like John Ngu Foncha and Augustine Ngom Jua, all from the Bamenda Grassfields, bolted away and formed the KNDP (Rubin, 1971: 86-88; Ardener,1962:348; Johnson, 1970:103-106).

It was because of Endeley's vacillating character which caused Foncha and Jua to bolt away from the KNC in 1955 to form the KNDP. The KNDP campaigned for secession from Nigeria and reunification with French Cameroun. The KNDP in the Kom fondom was led by Augustine Ngom Jua and Echi Kinni who used various ways as well as traditional organisations to eclipse the KNC. One of these was the *Anlu*, and this was precisely how the *Anlu* became a player in British Southern Cameroons politics. The KNDP leaders, especially Jua, were more shrewd, sensitive and unassuming in the observances of traditional norms, which they used to their benefit, than the KNC leaders (For more on the formation of the KNC and KNDP and the functioning of political parties in the Southern Cameroons (see LeVine,1964:193-214; Ardener,1996:290-294; Ngoh, 2001:92 - 96: Mbile, 2000: 94-122; Nkwi, 1985 :189).The KNDP politicians used the *Anlu* during the 1958 demonstrations to gain votes in the January 1959 elections while the latter used the former to settle old scores.

## The *Anlu* 'Revolt'

The *Anlu* revolt of 1958 had both remote and immediate causes. One of the remote causes of the 1958 *Anlu* uprising centred on the farmer-grazier conflict. The cattle destroyed the farmers' crops. The farmers, especially women, wanted the KNC government to protect their crops against destruction by the cattle owned by the Fulani. The KNDP gave the women the impression that the KNC government was incapable of doing so especially as women whose crops were destroyed were not usually compensated (Nkwi, 1976: 176).

23

Rumour had it that the Fon was about to sell Kom land to the KNC leader, E.M.L. Endeley, and to the Igbos (Jonson, 1970:367). It was also rumoured that grass which was used for roofing houses in Kom would be sold after December 1957. These rumours were further compounded and complicated by the enforcement of the cross-contour regulation by a non-Kom agricultural assistant, Joseph Ndikum. To say that the KNC was conniving with E.M.L. Endeley to sell Kom land was enough to invite trouble because land in Kom was considered sacred and the KNDP leadership knew it.

Furthermore, the role of the missionaries in Kom aroused the consciousness of the women who finally revolted in 1958. According to de Vries (1998:2) the influence of Christianity in Kom was so far-reaching and profound that virtually no aspect of Kom social and political life was left unaffected And as far as women were concern de Vries opined that The Missionary activities in Kom had radically changed the position of women by preaching "one man one wife" and also related issues of evangelisation. These preaching made the Kom women to become "aware" of their rights. But de Vries also did not realise in her fieldwork that even in pre-colonial Kom, women had power that could not be compromised following even the birth of *anlu* itself.

Njinikom, which was the theatre *of Anlu* revolt in 1958, was also the cockpit of Christianity. It was because of this that one cannot detach missionary activities in Kom from the *Anlu* revolt of 1958. But the immediate cause of the 1958 unrest was the agricultural policy which had been implemented in 1955. In that year, a regulation was passed enforcing contour ridging in areas such as Kom because of its mountainous nature. According to the regulation, linear ridges were to be constructed horizontally rather than the traditional vertical pattern; this was to check soil erosion. But what exactly was this agricultural law? The next section will turn to that law.

## Colonial Ordinances: Agricultural Law in Wum Division

The British colonial administration in most parts of Africa was obsessed with ordinances. One of those ordinances was about agriculture. The Southern Cameroons Agricultural Law of 1955 was captioned "A Law to Make Provision for Regulating the Planting and Growth of Agricultural Crops, for the Control of Plant, Diseases and Pests and for Matters Connected Therewith." This law was published in *Laws of the Southern Cameroons 1954, 1955 and 1956 Containing the Ordinances and Subsidiary Legislation of the Southern Cameroons*, and it is still lying at the National Archives Buea (NAB) Cameroon. Any individual who hindered or molested an Agricultural Officer or other person charged with implementing the law and who failed to furnish the required information was liable to either a fine of one hundred pounds or to six months imprisonment or both.

In actual fact, on July 21 1956, the Wum Divisional Authority Soil Conservation Rules were enacted to re-enforce the 1955 law. These rules contained eight main articles describing farm sizes, method of cultivation and restrictions to farmland. In article two for example, farms were to be divided by grass strips six feet wide across the slope on the line of the contour of the land into farming areas. In the fifth article, all cultivated ridges or beds in the farming areas were to be across the slope on the line of the contour of the land. The sixth article restricted farming within ten yards of any small stream, twenty yards of any large stream and thirty yards of any river bank. Those who contravened these rules were liable to a fine of up to ten pounds or two months imprisonment or both. These rules were approved and signed by J.O. Field, Commissioner of the Cameroons on 13 August 1956 and went into operation on 1October 1956. These rules are contained in *Laws of the Southern Cameroons 1954, 1955 and1956 containing the Ordinances and Subsidiary Legislation of the Southern Cameroons*, NAB.ds of Cameroon. (Also see, File Mi/b (1955)1, Soil conservation orders and rules made by N.A. Bamenda Division).

This ordinance as excellent as it sounded the colonial administration failed to take off time to educate the women. Instead in 1958, the Agricultural Department enforced the regulation without sensitizing the women on the merit of the new technique. Fines were imposed on defaulters and corn, beans and potatoes were uprooted by the Agricultural Assistant, Joseph Ndikum, in Anjin (Personal communication with Interview Prince Henry Mbain, Buea Town, 28 August 1999; Nawain Alice Chia, Buea 14 September 1999). Vertical ridging had characterised Kom traditional method of farming for a very long time and according to the Kom, this symbolised *Abun-a-wain* (the ridge of the child). To radically ask them to change this method without taking pains to educate them was enough to cause trouble. To add salt to injuries, in July 1958 a meeting was held at Yindo Mbah's compound at Njinikom; Mbah was the head of Njinikom. The purpose of the meeting was to explain the *raison d'être* of the 1955 Agricultural Law. He was a KNC member and he explained that the law was enacted with the knowledge of all the political parties. What was more was that he insisted that the law would not be repealed whatever the situation (Interview with C.K. Barth, Njinikom, 15 July 2000; Angela Musi Interview at Njinikom, 21 July 2000; Milne, 1999: 380).

Three issues draw our attention here. Firstly, why is it that a law passed in 1955 was only revisited in July 1958? Secondly, if the law was promulgated with the consent of all the parties, why did C.K. Barth in 1958 say that it could not be repealed? And finally, the KNDP members who were present refused to associate themselves with the views expressed by the chairman of the Wum Divisional Council. This was an indication that the KNDP supported the women and preferred to watch the reaction of the KNC. As far as the Agricultural Law was concerned and the KNDP, Milne (1999:321) puts it lucidly "... the soil conservation Regulations had done harm and provided the KNDP and the *Anlu* with good opportunities to resist". What is important is that C.K. Barth's position that the Law was there to be obeyed and could not be changed sparked off the resistance with far-reaching ramification in Kom and in the of Southern Cameroons. The women reacted ferociously to this statement.

**Rebellion Begins**

Bartholomew Chia Kiyam was "put to flight" from the meeting by a group of angry women to the great pleasure of the KNDP members. As he made his way to the mission compound, the women sang and danced and as their emotions and sentiments grew, they decreed that he was no more their son and added, "he was excreta". The first major mass demonstration took place in Njinikom on 8 July 1958, and drew .women from every part of the Kom fondom. It was on this day that the women asked for the removal of the KNC teachers at the Njinikom primary school because, according to them, "all their troubles" were due to the KNC government. Therefore their demands showed that the KNDP was the brain behind the women's demonstrations. These events occurred as the KNC leader, Dr. Endeley, had planned to visit Kom. Endeley made his visit to Kom on 11 July 1958 despite warnings from Augustine Ngom Jua that he should cancel it. Jua, probably never wanted Endeley because Endeley would have dismissed the rumours spread by him and the KNDP. Travelling from Wum to Njinikom, the premier and his entourage came across several "barricades" set up by the women.

On arrival at Njinikom, they met only a few supporters. The *Anlu* had succeeded in intimidating the men from attending the meeting with the premier. Furthermore, demonstrations and reports of mock-burials of KNC leaders by the *Anlu* gave the impression that those who supported the KNC would be punished, supernaturally. Joseph Ndong Nkwain's sudden death on 21 December 1958 was attributed to *Anlu*. Although informants hold divergent views about the cause of his sudden death, an archival document found in the Wum Divisional archives seems to bring us out of this huddle (confidential Medical Department, File N°25 E. 28/C. F:28/C. 7. Vol. I Divisional Archives , Wum).

The *Anlu* revolt did not continue *sine die*. It attracted the cream of colonial administration in British Southern Cameroons.

### The Reaction of the British Colonial Administration

On 14 July 1958, the Divisional Officer of Bamenda Division, Ken Shaddock, attended a mass rally at Njinikom market square in order to listen to the grievances of the women and pacify them. But the demonstrations were so wild that no effective meeting took place. Fon Alo'o Ndiforngu of Kom was virtually powerless because he could not control the women and he was frequently called by name, a taboo in the fondom. The *kwifoyn,* an executive arm of the Fon, remained completely aloof. *Anlu* had taken over the Kingdom. When Shaddock was holding the meeting with the women at the Njinikom market square, his interpreter was not telling the women what the D.O was saying. One of the women whose name was Helen Kikii noticed that and called the attention of the DO by raising her finger to inform the DO that the interpreter was not translating what the DO was telling the women.

Helen was born around 1905 and went to the Native Authority School which was opened in Kom in 1924 as the first girl. After that she taught in the Adult school which was opened in Njinikom. In a personal communication with me she told me that on that day she raised her finger and asked the interpreter to the hearing of the D.O. why he was not telling the people what the DO was saying. The DO in turn now made him the interpreter. Through out the period of that revolution she played the role of an interpreter/ translator.

Towards the end of July 1958, the police decided to arrest the ringleaders but when they arrived, the *Anlu* leaders voluntarily gave themselves up and agreed to travel to Bamenda. This action led more than two thousand women to march to Bamenda. Given the tense atmosphere, the Commissioner of the Southern Cameroons, J.O. Field, dispatched his deputy, Malcolm Milne, to Bamenda to ascertain the seriousness of the "Kom troubles".

While in Bamenda, Milne met Ken Shaddock and the Superintendent of Police, Jones, and talked to the women who listened politely to what they had to say and that was "as far as they could go"(Milne, 1999: 380). It was difficult to take action against women who looked innocent and yet were prepared to go to prison. The government ordered the women to return to Kom and provided them with transport and food. Milne recommended that the police post at Njinikom should be increased to at least ten men and that the detachment should be provided with a Land Rover. He suggested that the Premier's Office should look at the early introduction of the Kom Clan Native Authority (Milne, 1999:381). Finally he demanded that the Agricultural Law should be suspended for the time being. It should be borne in mind that during the march to Bamenda, other women from Babanki, Bafut and Wum joined the Kom women because they shared a common grievance with them, the destruction of their crops by the Fulani cattle.

However, as far as the political scenario in the Kom fondom was concerned and with special regard to the "Long March" of the women to Bamenda, thirty-seven men, all KNDP supporters, identified themselves with the *Anlu* and acted more or less as their advisers. Augustine Ngom Jua was one of the thirty-seven men and he advised them and provided them with drugs to calm their pains

(Personal communication with Veronica Bongbi, Njinikom, 10 November 1999). By doing this, Jua probably anticipated using the *Anlu* to achieve his political ends. Similarly, the *Anlu* women equally saw Jua as a "saviour" who was to redress their grievances, especially concerning the cross-contour farming. The crux of the matter is who used who? Was it Jua who used the *Anlu* or the *Anlu* who used Jua? While Jua was shuttling between Nkwen and Baingo arranging for the lodging of the *Anlu* women, his wife, Madam Nathalia Noh Jua, was equally busy supporting the women in her own way, and her role in boosting the *Anlu's* morals cannot be underscored.

### The Role of Madam Nathalia Jua Noh

Madam Nathalia Jua Noh was born in Njinikom in 1928. She became Jua's wife in 1951. She underwent elementary education from 1941 to 1947. She was a teacher in St. Anthony's primary school, Njinikom in 1958. At the outbreak of *Anlu* in 1958, she had given birth to their first son. Bernard Nantang and she had a second pregnancy. Madam Jua covertly supported the *Anlu* because she was pregnant and pregnant women were excluded from actively participating in the *Anlu*. In view of this, she began by covertly supporting the *Anlu*. When the women invaded the St. Anthony's Primary School, Njinikom, to demand the transfer of the KNC teachers, she carefully "slipped off' and sat under the church bell which was just a few metres from the school (personal communication, Njinikom General Hospital 7 September 2001)

After the women had finished their assignment, they met her "comfortably" seated under the bell house. "Nawain you never went to school, today?" The women asked her and she replied that she could not go to teach in school when they (the women) were in trouble (Personal Communication with Nathalia Jua, Njinikom Hospital, 8 September 2001). By saying so it meant, directly or indirectly, that she was in support of the course the women were fighting for. Her role became clearer during the women's trek to Bamenda. During that "Long March," she parcelled foodstuff and money for the women, and gave them garri, bananas and £2(Personal Communication with Anna Ayumchua who was one of the spies, Njinikom 20 December 2002) All these gifts were referred to as *Ayum a'gwesii anlu* (anything that was given in support of *Anlu*). The fact that this gesture was shown towards *Anlu* by Jua's wife indicated, first and foremost, how she was committed to the cause of the women and how their morals were boosted.

If the adage "Behind every successful man there is a woman" is anything to go by, Jua's wife did just that for her husband. According to her when her husband worked hard during the day with "those *Anlu* women" especially during their trek to Bamenda, she ensured that his food and warm water for a bath were always available. Although during an interview with her she did not clearly state her anticipated gains, it is evident that she nursed the ambition of becoming somebody higher when the husband moved to a higher political grade. This was manifested when the January 1959 elections approached; she used her two sisters to influence their husbands and family members who had reached the voting age to vote in favour of the KNDP. She made them to understand that should the KNDP win the elections, "it will be good news to the family."[35] This meant that if her position changed for the better, the family standard of living would also change.

## The KNDP and the *Anlu*

The KNDP leaders resorted to *Anlu* because they wanted to derail the KNC in Kom and win the January 1959 elections. The KNC was firmly entrenched in Kom under the unassuming leadership of Joseph Ndong Nkwain who lived and "died for it." Between 1953,and 1957, the KNC commanded a strong following in Kom where it had a majority of representations in the Kom Clan Council and in the Wum Divisional Council. To win an election in Kom against the KNC required complete revolutionary measures (Nkwi, 1976:186). The KNDP leaders, Jua and Echi Kinni, were aware of this.

One of the reasons for the KNDP's large following in Kom after 1958 was the personality and the intelligence of Augustine Ngom Jua and Kinni, as well as the KNDP platform. It should be recalled that the immediate cause of the 1958 *Anlu* insurgence was "the cross contour farming" regulation which was promulgated in 1955 by all political factions in the Wum Divisional Council. The members of that council must have been educated enough to understand the reasons for soil conservation. The fact that the KNDP leaders knew the reasons for the promulgation of the law, but went ahead and fabricated rumours about the sale of Kom land and played on the shortcomings of the ignorant and "illiterate" women showed how "smart" and forceful they were in pursuing their political ambitions. During the march of the women to Bamenda, Jua worked tirelessly to arrange for their lodging in Bamenda and when this author asked why Jua worked so hard, Anna Ayumchua responded in a song: Old women, let us not hurry, we should go gradually because Jua is at Nkwen arranging for our lodging (Personal communication in which the informant sang the song.. 20 December 2001).

She added that Jua provided them with some "whiteman's medicines", probably this must have been "pain-killer" drugs, to relax their muscles in the course of trekking to Bamenda, Above all, Jua's statement to LeVine in 1965 that he owed everything to the fortuitous actions of the *Anlu* in July 1958 goes to confirm the fact that the KNDP used *Anlu* to achieve its desired ends Ritzenthaler,1960:483; LeVine,1964;1963; 1964) Foncha and Jua knew that if they had to survive in the political scene, they had to appeal to regional and tribal sentiments. They built up grassroots support by weaving their nationalist ideas with traditional values. Besides, Foncha showed a lot of humility towards the Fons of the Grassfields and as a result wooed them (For more on this, see Rubin, 1971: 87; Milne, 1999:380). It was because of this manipulation and what the *Anlu* anticipated to gain that in January 1959, the *Anlu* came out massively to campaign and convince pro - KNC militants to vote for the KNDP.

**The *Anlu* and the 1959 Elections**
The Southern Cameroons House of Assembly was dissolved on 23 December 1958 in preparation for the 24 January 1959 general elections. Those who were qualified to vote were British subjects or British protected persons who were indigenes of the Southern Cameroons for a continuous period of not less than twelve months before the qualifying date. As far as the 1959 elections and the *Anlu* were concerned, directives on how to vote came from *Muana* and *Fuam*. The women who had gained the right to vote, voted massively for the KNDP. It should be recalled that the number of women who left Kom for Bamenda was estimated at between 2,000

**31**

and 6,000. On their way, they were joined by women from Bafut, Oku, Bu, Babanki, Bafmeng, Nkwen and Mankon. Some of these women saw in the *Anlu* a way of disengaging KNC activities from their respective areas. This was more so because if they supported *Anlu* it meant that they were supporting the KNDP. An example of these women was those of Bu and Befang. These were KNC strongholds and the women saw in *Anlu* a way to cast off the KNC yoke. (Interview with Mamma Cheng Beng, Bu (Wum), 18 October 2000. This view was further confirmed by Pa Beng George, interviewed at Befang, 25 November 2000.) Other women from Babanki, Bafmeng and Oku during my interviews attested to the view that they were angry with the KNC government, because it could not solve their problem with regard to the destruction of their crops by Fulani cattle. The Babanki women had an additional grievance: their land was used by their Fon to graze royal goats known as "Bongs!". They saw in *Anlu* a way to redress this grievance.

*The two women in the photograph were Anlu officers who were known as "Queen" (Fuam) and "District Officer" (Muana) These two officers lived at Wombong where, with the help of Kinni they directed the activities of the "New" Anlu.*

If the women joined the *Anlu* to Bamenda and became part and parcel of *Anlu*, it meant that they took orders from the *Anlu* "Queen" and "D.O." They sent out a communiqué from the *Anlu* headquarters, Wombong, emphasizing that all the women and their husbands who had attained voting-age should vote for the KNDP. When *Muana* was asked why she laid a lot of emphasis on the KNDP, she replied that it was Jua's party and this was the only way they (the *Anlu*) could reward Jua for what he had done to them since the *Anlu* resistance began in the fondom and added that Jua was their son. The *Anlu* used songs as one of their campaign strategies to send across their pro-KNDP messages. One of the songs ran thus:

Ngam Nkuoh lies in the earth, No! He did not sell the land. Ndong Nyang has come to sell the land. Ndi Nkuoh lies in the earth, No! He did not sell the land, Ghajem has come to sell the land...

Ngam Nkuoh and Ndi Nkuoh were both late fons whom the *Anlu* was paying tribute for never tampering with, or selling their land while they were alive. Ndong Nyang was the name of late Joseph Nkwain, the pilot of the KNC plane in Kom. Ghajem was the nickname of C.K. Bartholomew, the chairman of the Wum Divisional Council and a member of the KNC in Kom.

From the song, it was evident that the *Anlu* was campaigning for the KNDP Ndong Nyang and Ghajem were pillars of the KNC in Kom and the women took their flaws to contrast it with the virtuous fons, Ngam and Ndi Kuoh. Another song used by the *Anlu* to campaign in Kom was the song they had sang while on their way to Bamenda. The wordings were:

Mothers don't hurry, please don't Echi pleads at Bamenda
Please don't worry, don't hurry
Mothers don't hurry, please don't, Jua pleads at Bamenda
Please don't worry, don't hurry

This song portrayed the relentless efforts employed by the KNDP politicians during the *Anlu 's* "Long March" to Bamenda. During that event, Jua and Echi shuttled between Bamenda and Kom, making arrangements for the lodging of the women at Bamenda and providing them with some "pain killer" drugs to relax their muscles as earlier explained. However, this was not enough to show where the *Anlu* wanted the electorate to cast their vote. What was more was that after singing this song, the women ended up asking a question in chorus, "Jua and Echi what can we do for you people our dear sons?" With the elections at the doorsteps it was obvious that this was a request for a vote in favour of the KNDP. Another strategy which was used by the *Anlu* in 1959 was intimidation. According to Johnson, "... the women of Bikom [Kom] eventually set upon the compounds of KNC supporters, pressured their men into joining the KNDP under threat of denial of food and other services...."This method was also emulated by the women of Bu, Befang, Babanki, Bafmeng and Mankon, By doing so, the position of the KNC was weakened.

Finally, *Anlu* used her messengers *(gwe sa 'anlu)* who were sent to the entire neighbourhood of Kom and beyond to sensitise the populace on the 1959 elections and Jua. They were instructed to say that Jua was contesting the upcoming elections against Endeley. The hatred for the KNC and Endeley had eaten deep in the minds of the Kom given that the KNDP politicians had spread the rumour that Endeley was coming to take their land and sell it to the Igbos. The women, in particular, had developed a phobia against the KNC because the government was reluctant to provide a solution to their crops which had been destroyed by the Fulani cattle. Finally, the cross contour farming law was obnoxious to the traditional method of farming. The KNC government was held responsible for promulgating that law. All these had brought the fury of women and some men in Kom and beyond against the KNC and, of course, Premier, Endeley. It was because of all these that the political pendulum swung in Jua's favour and the KNDP.

As at 1 January 1959, *Anlu* had prepared the Kom constituency for the 24 January 1959 elections. When the votes were finally counted, out of the twenty-six seats in the House of Assembly, the KNDP captured fourteen while the KNC - KPP alliance had twelve. The votes were 75,326 for the KNDP and 52,425 for the KNC-KPP alliance.; Le Vine, (File N° Vale 1958/2 "Southern Cameroons House of Assembly elections, 1959")

In Wum East where the Kom constituency was found, out of a total of 4,469 registered voters, 3,263 voted for the KNDP while only 453 voted for the KNC-KPP alliance. To further show how the march of the 2,000-6,000 women to Bamenda in 1958 affected the 1959 elections in the Bamenda and Wum Divisions, it is necessary to look at Table I.

**Table I:    1959 Southern Cameroon's Election Bamenda and Wum Division**

| Constituency | Registered voters | KNC/KPP voters | KNDP/OK | Independent |
|---|---|---|---|---|
| **Bamenda** | | | | |
| North | 10793 | 3083 | 2879 | 269 |
| East | 5736 | 462 | 3239 | |
| Central West | 7746 | 462 | 5736 | |
| Central East | 10423 | 725 | 4937; 144 | 133 |
| West | 12950 | 1595 | 0 | 79 |
| South | 15932 | 166 | 7478 | 6908 |
| | | | 5929 | |
| **Wum** | | | | |
| North | 3709 | 1410 | 1031 | 736 |
| Central | 4234 | 1442 | 1398 | |
| East | 4469 | 453 | 3263 | |
| West | 2621 | 769 | 1079 | |

*Source:* Victor Julius Ngoh, *Cameroon 1884 - 1885: A Hundred Years of History* (Yaounde: Navi Group Publication, 1987), 211.

From Table I, it is evident that the KNDP scored spectacular victories in Bamenda and Wum Divisions. For instance, in the Bamenda Central West, where Babanki was found, out of 7,746 registered voters, 3,239 voted for the KNDP and only 473 voted for the KNC/KPP. It should be remembered that the Babanki women joined the *Anlu* women to Bamenda and *ipso facto* had an impact on the number of votes in favour of the KNDP. The effect was even greater in Wum Central, a traditional KNC fief, and Wum West. In Wum Central, the narrow win of the KNC - 1,442 votes as against 1,398 for the KNDP was due to the influence of the *Anlu* in some of the villages like Bu. For Wum West, the votes of Befang contributed in tilting the balance in favour of the KNDP. The election results revealed that the KNDP pulled 1,079 votes as against 769 for the KNC.

The KNDP victory of 14 seats to twelve for the KNC - KPP alliance was not however, very convincing and decisive. As a matter of fact, the KNDP won because of the tactical blunder which the KNC - KPP alliance committed. In Wum North, the KNC fielded an independent candidate and split the 1,295 votes while the KNDP candidate won with 1,031 votes. What obviously was the weakest blunder manifested by the KPP - KNC alliance was the fielding of Independent candidates. (Vc/1958/2 West Cameroon House of Assembly Elections Reports).

The men voted due to several reasons. Firstly, they were pressured by their wives. Secondly, the KNDP platform was appealing to them and finally, the personal ties of Jua and Echi attracted them. Yet some women still held on strongly and voted for the KNC. Various schools of thought hold divergent views as to why women voted for the KNC. One school of thought maintains that some women did not want to oppose their husbands. They further maintain that they did not want to go against the established traditional norms of the society (Confidential file N° 465, Wum Divisional archives, Wum.) Others hold the view that their relatives held lucrative positions in the KNC government and they did not want to jeopardize that by joining the KNDP (Personal communication with Thomas Mai, Njinikom, 30 April 1998) Besides, some women voted for the KNDP not because they had wished to do so but because Ndong Nyang's dead forced them to do so (Personal communication with Yindo Mbah, at Njinikom, 30 June 1999) Whatever the case, Jua captured the only KNDP seat in the Kom constituency. On 30 January 1959, Foncha, the president of the KNDP, became Premier of the Southern Cameroons.

The long dream of the KNDP of coming to power or derailing the KNC was transformed into a reality. Although it cannot be stated that the victory of the KNDP in the Bamenda and Wum Divisions was solely the work of *Anlu per se,* there is no doubt that from the above analysis, it influenced the outcome of the 1959 elections, at least in the Kom fondom. If about 2,000 women came from Kom during the Bamenda trek, and threw in their lot with the KNDP and taking into consideration that other neighbouring villages joined them, it is within reason to conclude that the *Anlu* contributed in influencing the outcome of the 1959 elections.

The importance *of Anlu* was felt more when the election results only showed a narrow margin. It was 14 seats for the KNDP and 12 seats for the KNC. The situation would have been more precarious for the KNDP had it been *Anlu* was absent when J.M. Boja, a KNDP member of parliament from Wum West, crossed the floor to the KNC on 11 March 1961 (Mbile, 2000:141) After Boja's deflection, the House of Assembly was evenly split with the KNDP having 13 seats and the KNC/KPP alliance 13 seats. The "13-13 balance" in the house meant that any additional crossing of the carpet from the KNDP would have led to the formation of a government by the KNC or the calling of fresh elections.

That notwithstanding, it is still a puzzle whether the *Anlu* women had noticed that they had been used by the KNDP politicians. According to the *Anlu*, they had gained by following the KNDP. This was because the cross-contour farming was suspended, thanks to the KNDP politicians of the Kom constituency. The KNDP, on the other hand, used the *Anlu* to capture a seat in the 1959 elections. The crux of the matter was who had used who? To say the least, the KNDP used the *Anlu* and the *Anlu* used the KNDP but as the situation later on showed in 1961, the KNDP used *Anlu* more.

## The *Anlu* Dilemma in 1961

The *Anlu* did not end with the Bamenda trek nor did it end with the KNDP victory in the January 1959 elections. After the KNDP victory, Jua moved to the regional capital, Buea, and the *Anlu* sent him £65 from their treasury. This gift, known as *alangha-wain* (the child's food), was the filial gesture of Kom women towards the son they had helped to bring to power (Nkwi,1976:98). But no sooner had the *Anlu* displayed this filial gesture than the KNDP government started distancing itself from them. The *Anlu* resistance was sparked off because of the cross-contour farming regulation. The law was suspended for a while by the colonial administration. It was later upheld and reinstated, this time with a difference by the KNDP government. Agricultural agents were sent to the field to educate the women on the advantages of soil conservation and those who constructed the cross-contour ridges were given an incentive in the form of a new hoe.

Apart from reinstating the cross-contour regulation, in 1960 thirty-seven *Anlu* women who had destroyed the ridges of some women because they were anti-KNDP were taken to the Bamenda court. The *Anlu* women thought that the KNDP government was going to protect them but to their chagrin, they were judged found guilty and fined. Was this the government which the *Anlu* campaigned vigorously to bring to power in 1959? Was this the government to whom they had sent £83 in early 1960? These questions did not only give the *Anlu* a sense of frustration but placed the women in a more confused situation. The KNDP government further distanced itself from the *Anlu* when it promulgated Decree 61-DF-23 of 6 November 1961, stating that no disorder would be tolerated and that defaulters would be dealt with accordingly. The embarrassment *of Anlu* was complete and by the end of 1961, *Anlu* had petered out as a political force in the Kom fondom.

## Conclusion

The *Anlu,* a traditional women's institution which was aimed at redressing grievances committed against women by men and vice versa in the Kom fondom of the Southern Cameroons, effectively assumed a political function in 1959. This was made possible by the KNDP politicians who used it to unseat the governing KNC which was firmly entrenched in Kom. The KNDP did so by spreading rumours calculated to woo the women who, anticipating gaining by following the KNDP, campaigned and contributed in influencing the outcome of the January 1959 elections in the Kom Fondom and certainly in its environs. This was exactly what the KNDP politicians had anticipated. The KNDP wooed the women and in 1959 elections the KNDP won the elections although by a slim margin of 14-12. The KNDP formed the government and shaped the political destiny of the Southern Cameroons. By 1961, however, and in only less than three years of its successful 1958 resistance, the anlu had collapse as a political force to be reckoned with in the Kom Fondom. The next chapter will turn its attention to songs from Kom. These songs show in a way the reflexivity and creativity of the Kom people and how even the voiceless could contribute towards alternative sources of history.

# Chapter Three

## Folk-songs and History among the Kom of Northwest Cameroon

### Introduction

This chapter foregrounds orality as a powerful route into the history and memory of societies whose history has been marginalized in the written word with focus on the Kom Fondom of North West Cameroon. The importance of oral sources in the construction of African history has been coalesced by many years of debates, postulation, and acceptance. Many researches have authenticated the feasibility and therapeutic efficacy of the uses of this genre of sources in reconstructing history (Amutabi, 2002: 192). Africanists and African scholars who first championed oral sources as a foundation of history include Thomas Hodgkin, Basil Davidson, Terence Ranger, Philip Curtin, Steven Feierman, Leonard Thompson, Jan Vansina, Kenneth Onwuka Dike and B. A. Ogot.

It was Melville Herskovits, a renowned anthropologist who first advocated the role of oral transmission, when he pointed to the surviving aspects of African culture among the New World Africans in the Diaspora in what he called "cultural tenacity" (Freud, 1998: 8). Certain aspects of culture that existed in African societies were still prevalent among the Africans in the Americas, especially music and aspects of language. It was for this reason that the place of music became central in historical reconstruction in Africa.

Over the past decades, visual as well as non-visual sources have evolved as powerful means of gaining access to alternative histories. It is increasingly acknowledged that non-visual and visual records, whether art or documentary, offer new routes to the past, especially where the life experiences and expression of people in most societies have been marginalized in the conventional dominant written word. This chapter will show how orality (folk-songs or people's songs) amongst the Kom of Northwest Cameroon can be used as an alternative source of history. The significance of this chapter lies in the fact that this source of history has not been adequately handled by Cameroonian scholars and researchers that have worked in the

Kom fondom (Chilver and Kaberry, 1967; Nkwi, 1976; Nkwi and Warmer 1982; de Vries 1991; Gam Nkwi, 2005) This chapter therefore is a contribution towards the utilization of orality in the historical reconstruction of the Kom.

Folk songs comprise the poetry and music of groups whose literature is perpetuated not by writing and print, but through oral tradition (Maria Leach 1950: 1032). These groups, primarily rural, are better able to preserve some of the older cultures of the national unit of which they form a part than the population of the cities with its more sophisticated, more international civilization, which is subjected to faster changes and fluctuations of fashion. Folk song could thus be considered as part of folk culture.

It is important to note from the onset that songs, as forms of recording and preserving history are not just confined to societies whose histories have been marginalized in written sources. Songs such as Australia's "Waltzing Matilda," England's "London is Burning," and Quincy Jones's "We are the World" (from the album *USA for Africa*) remind us of certain historical moments. Poet Benjo Paterson composed "Waltzing Matilda" in January 1895, against the backdrop of great labour strikes on Australian ranges that occurred between 1890 and 1894. This song was so effective in capturing the mood of the time that it was sung for the Prime Minister of Queensland on April 6, 1895 (Amutabi 2002: 196). The same song was sung at the summer 2000 Olympic Games in Sydney with the same words.

England was almost bombarded into submission by German warplanes in 1940 during the Second World War and some parts of the city were burned as a result of the bombardment. The song, "London is Burning", that developed out of this historical event has survived many years. The song "We Are the World" from the album *(USA for Africa,)* composed by Quincy Jones brings to memory the Sahelian drought of 1984. The song brought together megastars like Stevie Wonder, Michael Jackson and Harry Belafonte in raising funds for famine-ravaged Africans in 1986.

The manner in which music is produced and consumed in Africa shows that they are products of particular events and as a result, serve various functions in respective societies. Finnegan (1970:272-28) provides some illuminating functions of songs. According to

**40**

her, songs could be used to report and comment on current affairs, for mounting political pressure, for propaganda and to reflect and mould opinion. At the local level, public singing performs the same roles as the press, radio and other types of publications in expressing public opinion and bringing pressure to bear on individuals. Songs could be an indirect means of communicating with rulers whom the singer hopes to influence while at the same time avoiding the open danger of direct speech. Butake (1978:138) maintains that the African manifests his feelings through an outburst of song when he loves and when he hates, when he works and when he plays, when he is at peace and when he fights, when a child is born and when dead takes its toll.

In many parts of Africa, history information has been transmitted through songs. Amutabi (2002:197) states that "Nkosi Sikele': Africa" which was composed at Lovedale Fort Hare University by the first black nationalist elite of South Africa, was sung by South Africans to agitate for their rights. Today it is one of the national anthems of South Africa, which reflects nationalist fervour. The tune has been adopted by many African nations including Tanzania and Zimbabwe. Coplan (1997) relates how Lesotho migrant labourers in South African mines have used their songs to show the apparent contradictions between the re-constituted past and the uncertain present. These migrant workers also used their songs to compare life at home and in the mines as well as family solidarity and long term separation. Vail and White (1997) show how in Mozambique, sugar plantation workers were able, through satirical songs to protest their suffering and preserve their identity. Pongweni (1997) shows how during the Zimbabwean war of liberation, Chimurenga music was appropriated and adapted from local traditions and the songs served to articulate the issues of the day more eloquently than any political speech or rally of the day.

In Cameroon, Nyamnjoh and Fokwang (2003) have put music in historical perspective with changing political regimes and rhetoric. The authors have argued that the content of political songs in Cameroon have changed with the fortunes or misfortunes of politics and politicians in high office. In another article (2005) Nyamnjoh and Fokwang examine the nexus between musicians and political power in Cameroon in order to understand the dynamics of agency and identity politics among musicians. They have also maintained and argued that politicians in Cameroon and indeed the rest of Africa have tended to appropriate musicians and their music in order to maintain themselves in power.

Among the Kom of Northwest Cameroon, songs reflect every aspect the people people's lives. The songs may portray diverse emotions such as anger, hatred, joy, gratitude, sorrow, anxiety and could also be used to mock individuals or groups of people. These songs also give expression to basic principles that underlie the social, political and cultural life of the people. They are also used during periods of mourning and the songs also treat political and social issues of contemporary Cameroon.

## The Evolution and Characteristics of Kom Folk-Songs

The evolution and subsequent development of Kom folk songs date back to the early years of the 19th century when the fondom was founded. (Bartholomew Nkwain, Personal communication, 10 February 2002). The songs evolved from the socio-cultural and political realities of the kom people and they started as forms of entertainment and gradually developed into an expression of rejection of negative social, cultural and political issues that surrounded the Kom and post-colonial Cameroon. The songs were stored in people's memories and were usually provoked by various events. Such events could either be pleasant or unpleasant.

These songs may express anger, hatred, joy, gratitude, lamentation or sorrow and could also be used to lampoon. By the same token, they are also used to shower encomiums on individuals whose activities in the community have been outstanding. The songs are not handed down like oral tales but rather, they are most often impromptu, and again could utilize symbols held by the kom people in high esteem.

The most popular of these songs are *"Njang wayn"* (birth songs); *"chong Fuli"* (friction drum society of Fuli); *"Njang Songbe"* (the song of Songbe's compound); and *"Ndong Ibozu"* (the horn society of Ibozu). This chapter will analyse these various types of songs, which are spontaneous compositions as opposed to those stored up in the memories of the people. They arise from personal experiences and document recent issues. Each important occasion in the life of the kom is an opportunity to compose songs.

In the performance of Kom folk songs there is little or no gender boundary. The only exception to the rule is the "chong" society, which is predominantly male, but as far as dancing is concerned both men and women participate. The *"ndong Ibozu"* group is made up of men and women who are in their middle ages. The *"njang Songbe"* group was formerly known to be the private fief of women, but as time evolved, men became actively involved (Yindo Fulani, Personal Communication, 30th March 2002). These groups have programmes that bring friends together in social interaction. The programmes also serve as forums for learning and exchange of ideas where new songs are discussed and practiced. In the next section, the songs will be discussed thematically and chronologically. They will also be categorized into pre-colonial and post-colonial periods.

### The Pre-colonial Period
These are songs that predate colonialism in the fondom. The main ideas embedded in these songs however cut across the periods.

#### Song 1: Culture in Transition
Kom you are happy
Saying that "fon Kom" is no more
Remove one stone from the triside hearthstones
And you will see a new side (3x)

This song is alluding to the fact that the kom has refused to pay allegiance and respect to the Fon of kom. The Fon is the ruler of the fondom and it is widely believed that he is semi divine and could perform quasi - religious functions in the fondom. He is supposed to command unalloyed respect. Instead they (the kom) are rejoicing at his demise. Several variables could explain why the kom has refused to give to its Fon the due respect. Amongst other things the introduction of Christianity in the first decade of the 20th century with its subsequent Western ideas made some of the early converts to look at Christianity for their salvation rather than the Fon whose functions had been semi-divine (de Vries, 1998). Cameroon, which was colonised by the Germans in 1884 (Rudin, 193 8) attracted labour force from the hinterland and the Kom was no exception. Those who went to work in the plantations returned home with a new culture, which also made them to lose respect of the Fon (Nkwi, 1976).

Furthermore, the song makes mention of removing 'one stone of the triside hearthstones'. Triside here refers to three sides and consequently announces the importance of numbers in Kom history. Three is a multivalent symbol and according to Shanklin, Contrary to Ferretti's erroneous assertion that eight is the most important number (1975: 24) the kom consider odd numbers as auspicious and even ones as inauspicious. Three is particularly important; adding this number to something gives it power. Three is a multivalent symbol signifying for example, the standard blessing invoking the three hands of Kom, the three hearthstones used for all domestic hearths and the three clans of Kom. (1976: 68) Ferretti's position may not be totally erroneous; neither is Shanklin's idea totally infallible. Rather, Ferretti could have said that eight was important, instead of saying that it was very important. The traditional Kom calendar has eight days and this is one reason why Ferretti described the number as very important.

Shanklin's use of the symbolisms of the three hands of Kom, three hearthstones used for all domestic hearths and the three clans of Kom" is correct but it will be too simplistic to leave it at that. The three hands of Kom or *Iwuu kom tual,* expresses the highest values of the kom (Mbi, 2004: 47) and means child, food and prosperity or *ghu wain, Afo-a-yina* and *nyamgvin,* respectively (Group Interview, Personal Communication, 30 June 2003). *Ghu wain* literally means child and calls for more birth and the increase of the Kom population and the promotion of lineage continuity. This means that every Kom man is expected to marry a wife and produce children. Living either as a celibate or as a bachelor all through one's life is unacceptable amongst the kom. Children are seen as a man's replica. When a man dies, it is believed that he continues to live on in his children (Bobe Minto, Personal Communication, 15, 16, and 17 June 2003).

*Afo-a-ayina* literally means uncooked food and refers to food crops such as cocoyam, plantain, sweet potatoes, maize, guinea corn, banana, beans, groundnuts etc. in modern parlance; this uncooked food is used interchangeably with cooked food (Ateh, 1976). *Nyam-ngvin* means prosperity. Learning a trade such as bricklaying, carpentry, plumbing was very important because it will bring in money, which will be used for the upkeep for the family and the kingdom (Nawain Anna Ayumchua, Personal Communication, 25 July, 2005).

Furthermore, the number three means the three founding clans of kom. According to oral data gathered and corroborated by Nkwi; 1976; Chilver and Kaberry, 1967, they were *Eku; Itinalah and Achaf*. The naming of these clans appeared to have originated from geographical homonyms. *Ikui* was derived from the family that was situated 'above' and *itinalah* was derived from 'below'. *Achaf* means a marshy area, which describes the third person's settlement. Three also could be seen as an important symbol in the most important sculpture of the Fondom, the *Afo-a-kom* (Gam Nkwi, 2005: 133-154). It was carved by Fon Yuh and it has three toes not five. This reverse of mammalian dimorphism was an indication of how important the number three is among the kom (Gam Nkwi; 2005:138).

### Song 2: Issues of Succession
You drove your brother and
Burnt the compound that
Plantains shall grow and decay
You drove your brother's wife
And his children
That they shall go to where?
Are you not ashamed?
Are you not ashamed?
Are you not ashamed?

Both matrilineal and patrilineal successions are practised in the Kom fondom and **Song** 2 dwells on this issue. Succession among the kom is always characterised by tension and kin competition. According to Kom oral tradition, Kom was a matrilineal society in which maternal nephews succeed uncles. After a man dies, the immediate next of kin is the deceased's brother who is code -named "caretaker". If he has five brothers, all of them will form a hierarchy of succession to him according to their ages. After this line, nephews could start to succeed their uncles. Some successors would send out the deceased's widows and children from the deceased's compound. In other instances, brothers would compete for the dead man's property.

In the last decades of the 20<sup>th</sup> century the kom who practice matrilineal succession have indicated that it was not auguring well within their social context For instance in 1972 the Kom elites in the Diaspora wrote an open letter to the Fon of Kom, Nsom Ngwe complaining bitterly that matrilineal succession retards development in Kom land. In reaction to this perceived anomaly, some kom people have decided to construct two compounds, one for their children and the other for the family (Bobe Kiing, Personal communication, 16 September 2004). Whatever the case, the patrilineal and matrilineal institutions are interwoven. The debate has further shown that people shape their institutions to suit their needs and do not uncritically obey tradition whatever the tradition may be.

### Song 3: Jua, the Popular Politician
Jua talked to the fon our father
'They have sent me to come and rest'
Jua said this, wrote a letter
'When you stay, look after the children
Death has overwhelmed me
It is my invitation that God has sent'.

This song begins with lamentation of the demise of a popular figure, Augustine Ngom Jua. The song states that Jua sent a message to the fon of Kom and the kom people, from the land of the dead.

Jua was born in Kom, Wum Division in 1924. After his education he took up teaching and then went into politics. In 1955 he helped to form the Kamerun National Democratic Party. In 1965, he was the West Cameroon Secretary of State for Finance and later became the Prime Minister of West Cameroon (1965-1968). He was a dynamic politician who was loved and respected by English-speaking Cameroonians in general and the kom in particular. His untimely death at the age of 53 in December 1977 seemed to have been a blow to the kom.

Certain things endeared Jua to the people. He is warmly remembered for his positive role during the Kom women riots of 1958-61. During the women's march to Bamenda, capital of Bamenda province, Jua expressed his solidarity by giving them painkiller drugs and arranging for their accommodation while in Bamenda. Although

Jua did all these things in anticipation of gaining votes in the 1959 elections, he however gained much popularity by supporting the women. This has already been handled in chapter one.

Within Southern Cameroonian circles, Jua was also popular. One of the fundamental factors, which accounted for this, was his life-long dedication to a better position for the Anglophone state of Cameroon, Before reunification, Jua's position, which was representative of that of the Kamerun National Democratic Party as a whole, was that Southern Cameroon must first sever its links with Nigeria and become an independent state in its own right before opening negotiations for reunification with French Cameroon on a federal basis. He emphasized the issues of integration and secession as the main issues in the plebiscite.

When Foncha, the head of the Kamerun National Democratic Party, (KNDP) in September 1959, at the United Nations agreed to substitute reunification for secession in the plebiscite, Jua wired him to indicate that the KNDP leadership considered such a compromise as unacceptable. Some schools of thought even maintain that Jua and his closest collaborators considered replacing Foncha as leader of the KNDP, after which they would rally support in the territory, and then pressure the UNDP into making secession versus integration issues at the plebiscite. But he was persuaded to abandon these plans when he was assured by the traditional rulers that Foncha would be able to secure reunification on the basis of a loose association or at worst a confederacy (Chem-Langhee, 1995:3). Jua demonstrated the extent to which he could confront the federal government in 1964 during Foncha's absence. Acting as deputy premier, Jua was alleged to have stopped the federal Inspector's car and forced him to remove the Cameroon flag that his car was flying. (Ade Ngwa, Personal communication, 20, August 2004).

It was based on the above antecedents that when Ahidjo visited West Cameroon on 11 May 1965 and in consultation with West Cameroonians, Jua was nominated as Premier of West Cameroon. Jua's ascendancy to the post of Prime Minister received the widest acclamation throughout the length and breadth of the territory, as he was the only one to respond to the much-needed reforms of the state, thus instilling hope and confidence in the people. The West Cameroon civil servants, in a message signed by its Secretary

General, N .N. Nsiong Enang, exhorted him to be the defender of the constitution and democracy and that he could equally transform "(the West Cameroon) into a socialist state beginning with the encouragement and setting up of farming schemes to check the influx of Youth from rural areas into cities" *(Cameroon Times,* vol. 5, No. 63, 18 May 1965:2). The women, whom Jua had sympathized with during their revolution, contributed £65 and sent to him as *alagn-a-wayn* (child's coco yam) (Gam Nkwi, 2003:172).

Jua's government was however rumoured to have crippled the Cameroon Bank, and this became a scandal *(Cameroon Times,* vol. 6, No. 23, 26-27 February 1966:1). This combined with his reluctance towards the adoption of a unitary state led to his fall from grace in 1968. The people however generously forgot these negative issues while composing the song in his honour.

### Song 4: The Lake Nyos Disaster
Fon Kom sent news to Paul Biya
An awful thing has happened in Nyos
Fon Kom sent news to Paul Biya
An awful thing has happened in Nyos (3x)

On 21 August 1986, Lake Nyos erupted, emitting poisonous carbon dioxide gas that had killed an estimated population of 10,000 people. The International Community reacted promptly and pumped in material and financial aid. Many other Nyos victims who had survived the disaster were herded into camps in different parts of the country. The Fon of Kom, Fon Njinabo II was advised in a song to send news to Paul Biya, the President of the Republic that something awful has happened in Nyos. The composers of this song equated the fon of the Kom state with Biya because they saw the Fon of Kom, as ruling the Kom state as well as Biya ruling Cameroon. Despite the aid that was provided for the lake Nyos victims, the story twenty years after, has remained a very sad one (Shanklin, 1992). Most of the victims are complaining that Biya's government has abandoned them mid-way and they wish to go back to Nyos (Ching Thomas, Personal Communication, 30th March 2006).

### Song 5: Election Rigging
O my son weep thou not
Father said he had nothing to spit
John Fru Ndi you stop crying
Children said, fraud defeated you (3x)

The song is meant to comfort a child that might have fallen down or has been hurt in one way or the other. In such instances, the parent usually spits into the child's hand for him/her to stop crying. During the 1992 Presidential elections in Cameroon in which John Fru Ndi was Paul Biya's running mate, it was alleged that the former won but the latter rigged the elections.

John Fru Ndi was born in July 1941 at Baba II, in Bamenda, present capital of the North West Province. As a Cameroons Peoples Democratic Movement Party, (CPDM) candidate, he contested the April 1988 Parliamentary elections on the Kaki ticket and lost (Ngoh, 1996). As co-founder of the Social Democratic Front Party (SDF) he officially launched the party, despite government's prohibition, on 26 May 1990. During the launch, law enforcement agents opened fire and killed six SDF sympathizers. A forceful and charismatic leader in his own right, he contested the October 1992 Presidential elections and came second.

He accused the incumbent of gross electoral malpractices and declared himself winner of the elections. In reaction, following Decree No. 92/003 of October 28, 1992, he was placed under house arrest and later released. As the national chairman of the SDF, he is one of the most popular politicians in Cameroon.

### Song 6: Retirement Benefit
When someone works for the government
On retirement, he is paid
Fuli, pay Chia "Ifel"
So that he should be trudging back to his "Ifel"

The song is asking Fuli, the geographical location of a royal compound in the southern sector of the Kom fondom to pay Chia *"Ifel"* so that he could go back *to* *"Ifel"*.

"*Ifel*" is the coded name of Bafut which is located to the West of the fondom. During the Kom wars of expansion which Fon Yuh waged on the neighbours to capture slaves one of the wars was with Bafut. In the course of the war slaves were captured and Chia was one of the slaves. While in Kom he was name Chia "*Ifel*" to denote that he was from Bafut, and he was living at the royal compound of Fuli. When Ndi vacated the compound to ascend the throne at Laikom, he kept Chia "*Ifel* to be the "caretaker" of the Fuli compound (Emmanuel Chia Nges, Personal communication 10 April 2006). This appeared to the Kom that, Chia would enter the royal line. To this effect and in total disagreement they composed a song asking Fuli to pay Chia "*Ifel*" so that he can go back to his native "*Ifel*" (Bafut). Just like any government worker who had served the state and was going on retirement and receives his retirement benefit Chia "*Ifel*" should be compensated.

### Song 7: Prostitution
Kom you have left a saying
They do not have a child in the house to send
While she had gone to Bamenda to prostitute
Kom you have left a saying
They do not have a child in the house to send
While she had gone to Bamenda to prostitute

The song indicates a social vice among the Kom, which is prostitution. Prostitution, according to the kom mind, is a new phenomenon and a colonial product. Colonialism created urban areas to facilitate administration and these urban areas came with social and economic amenities that were lacking in the rural areas. Rural dependents therefore saw something attractive to benefit from the cities. The net impact was that the kom teenage girls migrated to Bamenda, 64 kilometres away from Kom where they engaged themselves in the commercial sex trade. The impact of this rural-urban exodus was immediately felt in most Kom households. The song is lamenting that the girls who are supposed to be helping in most of the household chores and running errands for their parents are absent. In their absence, parents have become children in the households.

### Song 8: Paying Dowry

When someone visits his wife
In her parents compound
He goes home, sits down and prepares then sends the bride
price of his wife
Which kind of world is this, that somebody gives the bride price
of his wife
It is a bottle of beer?
He sits and drinks with his friends

The song narrates the traditional procedure of getting married to a wife amongst the kom during the pre-colonial period. The song, then suddenly breaks into rhetoric wondering what has caused the change in traditional practices. The song goes further to criticize fathers-in-law, who, rather than encouraging their son-in-laws, to pay the bride price, would merely demand beer from them in beer parlours.

The beginnings of capped brewed beer in Kom was directly link to the construction of the wider road and the geographical mobility of some of the Kom people. With the coming of the road, it marked the beginning of the waning of local liquor parlours especially in Njinkom known as *ndo kang* with some consequences. This does not in any way seduces us to think that *kang* houses never existed. They did in the villages but what was knew as far as the road was concern was that these *kang* houses moved to the roadsides or road junctions. The traditional liquor was brewed with corn which has been fermented for at least two weeks. It was then grind into powder and cooked. It took at least two days before it was fit for consumption. It was sold to people in traditional calabashes (*abali*). The sales were mostly done on traditional Sundays (*itu bole*) when people were not going for work to their farms. It was the beginning of socialisation between the Kom people in such new drinking spaces. In some *kang* houses often found in the market people came to meet and made friends. Men came to make *rendez-vous* with their love ones and others brought messages from the far interior and carry back messages to those who could not walk to the market.

In 1962, bottled alcoholic beer drinks came to be sold in Njinikom. The drinking parlour which served that purpose was known as Congo bar and was owned by Freeboy Mukong. I will now turn my attention to a history of the biography of Mukong and that bar. One of the eyewitnesses to the life history of Mukong was James Tubou.

Tubou was the eldest nephew of Freeboy Mukong was born in March 1935. At the age of 14 he already saw Mukong coming home on leave from the plantations. According to him Mukong was born around 1905 and he became one of the first recruits of the German plantations which was still at Mbwenga. Mukong worked in the Mbwenga plantations for more than ten years and when the CDC was created in 1946, PAMOL became a separate part of the same company. Because of the lack of labour, the management of PAMOL promised that anybody who will go to his home village and bring labour will be promoted to a higher rank and money paid to him according to the expenditure which he has incurred. It was on that note that Freeboy Mukong came home to Kom to recruit people. Fortunately for him, the people he brought were the most powerful as their output showed. At that time he was promoted to the rank of a headman and so much money too was given to him. He took part of the money and bought farms and planted his own farms.

When there was need for more labour he was always the one that was sent to go and bring more labour. He told Tobou that he did that thrice and the fourth time he was further promoted to the rank of an overseer. As an overseer now he controlled head men and labour. Most of the time now Mukong will divert labour to his farms and even when he went home for labour he recruited some of the labour for his farm. He worked with PAMOL for more than 25 years before he went on retirement in 1960. When he went on retirement he concentrated on his farms where he built two houses.

In November 1963 he was again hired to come home for labour. At that time Tubou was present and they went out together every morning to all the quarters of Kom. At the end of the day they had more than sixty people to take down to Ndian. Mukong told the recruits many stories that made them to be convinced that all in the coast was going to be fine and the people were going to have money. He even started by showing gratitude to the people by giving them money each day on the way. He will give a hundred francs each and if the people were to spend the night he will give them 200 Frs. each. That was much money. For those who had graduated from primary schools he will tell them that they will be employed as clerks, and some will be head men. He gave them all the promises and so trust was planted. And so he succeeded to take as many people as he could down to south. He did it until he came home finally in the mid 1980s.

Meanwhile as early as 1955 he had constructed this compound with stones and decided to open a drinking parlour in 1962 which was the first in Kom. People use to come from Belo, Fundong Anyajua to enjoy themselves in the bar.

## The Congo Bar

From the story above Mukong was able to open a bar because he was a recruiter of labour for the coastal plantations. The bar itself came into existence because the road was constructed to link Bamenda and Kom. The introduction of bottled beer was a novelty in Kom because people had been used to drinking only the *kang* which was not bottled. The beer was brewed in Douala in one of the first companies to specialise in beer production-*Brasseries du Cameroun* opened in 1959(For more on beer in Cameroon see Diduk, 1993:1-43; Schler, 2002:315-334).

In Kom the beer was given various names but the most common was (*muluh mi kfaang*) meaning the wine of newness. People had to travel from far places to come to Njinikom to buy and consume such beer because it became popular than the *kang*. One of the people who trekked to Njinikom for the consumption of the beer was Isaiah Megne. He was born in 1922 at Anjin Kom and he was a long-distance trader to Yola, Nigeria, Tiko, Victoria and Nkongsamba. He maintained that he had tasted *choumei* ( the name given to Beaufort beer by the Kom)in Nkongsamba and back in Kom he was tired to moved out for Nkongsamba he was always wondering where he could buy that beer. He was very happy to hear that beer was in Njinikom. He further maintained that beer tasted better than *kang*. He also took his closest friends to Njinikom(Personal communication with Isaiah Megne, Anjin, Kom 14 June 2008). From Megne we gather that the beer was better than the *kang* and that explains why he was consuming. In a similar situation in Abehema, Nyamnjoh (2009:151), observed that "nothing was as prestigious to the men of Abehema as beer brewed and capped in the cities. City beer offered them much-needed respite from the monotony of the local corn brew *kang*, which to them was definitely inferior to what came from the city in bottles firmly capped...." Those who drank the beer were those who felt that they were different from other people in terms of what was found in their wallets like their purchasing power. They also felt that they were consuming something new.

The beer also became popular amongst the Kom not only in terms of consumption but distribution in other areas of Kom. One of the people who played a significant role in the distribution of the beer was Zacheus Nchindo. He was born in 1940 at Aboh Kom and he finished his primary school in Cameroon Baptist primary school in Belo. After his primary school he moved over to Njinikom where he became a bar attendant in the Congo bar. According to him many people came from far interior areas and retail beer to carry it back to their hamlets. These people had just heard about the new beer and felt that they should consume it(Personal communication with Zacheus Nchindo, Aboh, 30 November 2008).The consumption of foreign things in peripheral societies has been noted by Miller(1995:150) in the following words: "societies on the periphery of the industrial world often seize readily upon new possibilities of consumption and use them to embody elements of modernity. This points to the fact that these new meanings do not only relate to the commodity and its consumption but also to the consumer's image" One of the first scholars to research beer in Cameroon, Susan Diduk attempted with much success to explain to the growing popularity of bottled beer. She also traced the distribution and marketing of the beer. From Njinikom the next bar was opened at Belo and Fundong. The opening of these beer parlours also led to the weakening of traditional loci ways of doing things. This is reflected in the women were dowried once beer has been introduced.

Of the offshoots of the introduction of beer was prostitution. This situation reflects the moral decadence that has pervaded Cameroon (Group of elders, Personal Communication 20th September 2005).

**Song 9: Infidelity**
You left your husband
Went and took a TRAPP
You left your husband
Went and took a TRAPP
You left you husband
Went and took a TRAPP
So that you could enjoy
Enjoy! Enjoy! Enjoy!

This song was composed when a German construction company constructed the Bambui-Fundong road with the abbreviation of TRAPP. During the construction of the road, many kom men were employed. Some wives also ran away to become concubines of other TRAPP workers who were not indigenous Kom. The women indulged in this nefarious act because of the social benefits which they anticipated gaining. (Group of Young men, Personal communication, 3$^{rd}$ October 2005). Others men also stated that they suspected that their wives had adulterous affairs with some of the TRAPP workers (Group of young men, Personal communication, 23 March 2006). According to most informants the situation of the road which was constructed since 1954 had deteriorated at a very fast rate in the 1990s, and did not only call for the attention of the Cameroon government but also international company. Many informants did not believe that it was the government who was responsible for the construction of the through a German company. This was mostly explained by the fact that people had loosed confidence in the government and felt that nothing good came from the government. Further research about the widening and re-construction of the road actually revealed to me that the Government of Cameroon through an agreement with the German government had secured some financial loans to the tune of DM 52,000,000. The agreement which was signed by Sardou Hayatou for the Government of the Republic of Cameroon and Friederich Reiche for the Government of Federal Republic of Germany went into effect on 3 on April 1987. The partial wordings of the agreements went as follows:

## Agreement 1
### Between the Governments of the Federal Republic of Germany and the Government of the Republic of Cameroon Concerning Financial Cooperation

The Government of the Federal Republic of Germany and

The Government of the Republic of Cameroon,

In the spirit of the friendly relations existing between the Federal Republic of Germany and the Republic of Cameroon,

Desiring to strengthen and enhance these friendly relations through financial Cooperation as partners,

Aware that the maintenance of these relations constitutes the basis of this Agreement,

Intending to contribute to social and economic development in Cameroon,

Have agreed as follows:

### Article 1
(1) The Government of the Federal Republic of Germany shall enable the Government of the Republic of Cameroon, or another recipient to be selected jointly by the two Governments, to obtain loans of up to a total of DM 52,000,000 (fifty-two million deutsche mark) from the Kreditanstalt für Wiederaufbau (Development Loan Corporation), Frankfurt am Main, for the "Bambui-Fundong road project", the "Kadey hydroelectric power station project", the "grain storage project" and the "Douala harbour project", provided that, on examination, the projects are considered deserving of support, and a financial contribution of up to a total of DM 3,000,000 (three million deutsche mark) for the "study fund III" project.

### Article 2
(1) The utilization of the amounts referred to in article 1 of this Agreement and the terms and conditions on which it is granted shall be governed by the contracts to be concluded between the Kreditanstalt für Wiederaufbau and the recipients of the loans and financial contribution; these contracts shall be subject to the laws and regulations applicable in the Federal Republic of Germany.

(2) The Government of the Republic of Cameroon, in so far as it is not itself a borrower, shall stand surety *vis-à-vis* the Kreditanstalt fiir Wiederaufbau for alldeutsche mark payments to be made in discharge of the borrower's obligations under the contracts to be concluded pursuant to paragraph 1.

It was on that basis that a German based company, *Groupement d'Énterprise Trap-Strabag Belfinger + Berger* which was shortened as TRAPP, was given the contract to construct the road. The company brought in their road equipment and most of their personnel from Germany and Italy. Following Article 3 "The Government of the Republic of Cameroon shall exempt the Kreditanstaltfiir fur Wiederaufbau (KFW) from all taxes and other fiscal charges levied in Cameroon ....." According to the *Wikipedia: The Free Encyclopedia*, KFW is German government owned development bank based in Frankfurt am Main. It provides funding for a wide variety of developmental projects throughout the major regions of the world. In other for the bank to justify her funding she undertook feasibility studies between Fundong and Bambui before the actual construction was undertaken.

The Bambui-Fundong road was justified on similar lines which had been justified in the 1920s and 1950s.

The Bambui – Fundong road gives the project region access to the central town of the region and to Cameroon's entire road network. The region and the agricultural sector in the catchment area of the road give the impression of activity. According to information provided by the local authorities there is no above-average migration away from the region. Agriculture seems to be very diversified and intensive and the surface where farming is possible due to the topography seems largely utilized. In socio-economic terms the Bambui – Fundong road has a positive impact on the target group since people now have a safer, considerably faster and cheaper access to the central town of Bamenda and its services. Moreover, the prices of goods imported into the region have declined markedly. Due to the Bamenda – Bambui road large parts of the North-West Province may now benefit from the positive effects generated by the better access to the administrative, social and health facilities of the administrative centre of Bamenda. The poor in the region are also likely to profit from the effects of the project. From today's point of view the project also has a positive impact on women, though the impact is not extraordinary. Any major environmental damage caused by the two roads cannot be identified. The environmental damage caused is usual for normal roads and considered as acceptable. With the reform of the transport system the road maintenance system and its financing was put on a fundamentally new and more efficient basis. The experience gained up to now with the new system is satisfactory. The opening up of the catchment area, which was the intention of the Bambui – Fundong road, has been achieved.

The Bamenda- Kom road like the old track radiates from Bamenda the provincial headquarters of the North West Region of Cameroon and extends 72.2 km to the western part of the region, reaching Fundong the administrative headquarters of Boyo division. The road covers a distance of 12 km from Bamenda to Bambui, 11 km from Bambui to Babanki, 25km from Babanki to Belo,8 km from Belo to Njinikom and 13km from Njinikom to Fundong. The construction of the road began in 1993 with many middle age men employed on the road at various capacities. Julius Aghaa Njua was one of the workers on the construction of the road. He was born in 1966 at Njinikom. He went to St. Anthony's primary school from 1973 to 1980. He obtained his First School Leaving Certificate and went St. Bede's college Ashing, Kom from 1981 to 1983. Julius further went to St. Augustine's college, Nso from 1984-1985. From 1985 to 1986 he continued to Kom Baptist Technical College where he read electrical engineering at a junior level. He told me that at the initial stage of the construction of the road, about 280 Cameroonians were employed as drivers, mechanics and other technical jobs, 15 German and 13 Italian engineers and by 1995 the number of labour had risen to well above 700 of which 276 were from Kom alone. Instead of the first phase of the road which the population used crude iron tools like hoes, pick axes and head pans the construction this time was quite mechanical. Caterpillars of all types, graders, were used.

It took close to five years for the road to be completed. The completion of the road in 1998 had economic and social consequences on the Kom people but our interest here is to examine how it affected geographical mobility. Obviously, with a tar road everybody will accept that the road resulted in exponential geographical mobility of the people in Kom. But that is just part of the story. The completion of the Bamenda-Kom road led to the opening of travelling bus agencies in Kom like Guarantee, Armour Mezam and Patience. These bus services or transport agencies transport people from Kom who went to areas beyond Bamenda, like Bafoussam, Limbe, Yaounde and Douala without having to stay in Bamenda as it used to happen. Goats, fowls, foodstuffs like plantains, bananas, corn, beans, potatoes, and carrots were sold in the Bamenda metropolis and even beyond.

## Conclusion

This chapter has shown the creativity of the subalterns in Kom in the way they produced songs and these songs on the other hand could be used as alternative sources for the reconstruction of history. The next chapter will examine boundary conflicts in Africa while taking the Bambili and Babanki-Tugoh as the case study.

# Chapter Four

# Boundary Conflicts in Africa:
## The Case of Bambili and Babanki Tungoh of Northwest Cameroon, c.1955-1998

## Introduction

This chapter sets out to investigate the causes of the Bambili and Babanki-Tungoh boundary conflict. It also examines the question of ownership of the land in conflict, manifestation of the conflict and attempts an appraisal of the conflict so far, while proffering some solutions aimed at solving this conflict. Both primary and secondary sources were consulted during this research and from the research the causes of the boundary conflict between Bambili and Babanki-Tungoh are many and varied and can be appreciated under social, economic and political domains. Recommendations have been made with the aim of providing a lasting solution to this perennial conflict.

The Berlin West African Conference (1884 - 1885), apparently signalled the creeping European economic and political dominance in Africa and accelerated its shift from informal to formal involvement in African politics. This led to the drawing up of artificial boundaries, which more or less authenticated various territorial claims by European powers, but, which also divided historically homogenous, contiguous and closely related, sometimes kinship communities. According to Asiwaju (1985:63), boundaries indicate the sharp edges of the territorial limits within which the states exercise their distinct jurisdictions'. They are therefore, the lines of contact, more often for conflict than for harmony, between rival systems of governmental control. A boundary could also be the line of delimitation or demarcation between administrative units or between geographical regions of various types. Three fundamental concepts underline the establishment of international boundaries. These are: the definition state, the delimitation and the demarcation stage. (Also see Boggs, 1940; Anene and Brown, 1966; Fanso,1989).

Since the attainment of political independence by most African countries in 1960 few, if any country, have not had cause to worry about the position of its boundaries in relation to its neighbours. Most of these boundary conflicts resulted from the separation of ethnic groups which hitherto then were considered as one single entity. For example, Somalia whose essentially continuous cultural area was severed into the separate colonies of British Somaliland, French Somaliland, Italian Somaliland, the Northern Frontier District of Kenya and the Ogaaden province of imperial Ethiopia; the Maasai cut nearly in half by the Kenya-Tanzania border; the Bokongo separated by the Gabon-Congo (Democratic Republic of the Congo-DRC) and DRC-Angola boundaries; and Lunda astride and DRC — Angola and DRC — Zambia frontiers; the Zande or the Azande cut by boundaries into different parts in the Sudan, Chad, the Central African Republic and DRC (Asiwaju, 1985: 176). The European powers embarked on the separation of these ethnic groups because of greed and egoism. What was uppermost in their minds was to get spheres of influences and this was motivated chiefly by economic, social and political considerations in what became popularly known in the second half of nineteenth century as imperialism.

Apart from the separation of these ethnic groups, almost all African countries have got boundary conflicts with their neighbours which, at times, have resulted in wars. For instance, Morocco resorted to war with Algeria to maintain the integrity of its boundaries over Western Sahara. Somalia claimed land from Ethiopia and Kenya over Ogaaden while Cameroon has not been in the best terms with Nigeria over the Bakassi Peninsular (Ghali and Asfahany, 1973; Prescott; 1971).

It was because of the arbitrary lumping of people and complete ignorance of ethnic composition of people by the Europeans that differences have occurred leading to inter village or ethnic crisis as well as crisis between states after attaining political independence. A case in point is the North West Region of Cameroon where inter-ethnic boundary conflicts have been common, since the beginning of the mid- twentieth century. For instance, the Bali-Nyonga has disputed with their neighbours over boundary issues at Barforchu and Chomba; the Balikumbat have contested with the Bafanji over their common border; the Oku have fought the Mbesa; the Bambui have clashed with the Funge and the Bambili. The epicentre of conflicts would however appear to be the Bambili and Babanki — Tungoh boundary conflict. Yet, in spite of this creeping malaise little, if any scholarly attention has been focused on this all important issue, its pernicious effects on neither the society nor withstanding. The goal of this paper is therefore to first, investigate the causes of the Bambili and Babanki — Tungoh boundary conflict and secondly, to show how this conflict can be considered as a product of the ever-empire-state-building process in the Bamenda Grassfields of Cameroon, while at the same time advancing some possible suggestions which if implemented will resolve the boundary feud.

## Staking the Landscape of the Study Area

The Bamenda Grassfields is located at the point where the long West African coastline turns sharply south to run down to the Congo and Cape. It is found east of the Greenwich, approximately between longitudes 5o3', and latitudes 9o5', 1' north of the equator. According to Chilver and Kaberry (1967:1-90), the Bamenda grassfields cover the former administrative divisions of Bamenda, Wum and Nkambe which in 1953 had a total population of 429,000 including 10.000 nomadic Fulani (mapl).

The dominant geographical feature of this area is the Bamenda High Plateau. It stretches from the North East and Fast of the Bamenda grasslands over the centre of the area at an average height of 4,500 feet above sea level. It is studded with peaks, the highest and most spectacular of them being the Akuofo Mountains between the Bamenda station and former French Cameroon frontier and the Oku Mountain which is 7,357 feet above sea level. The Bamenda plateau fall suddenly from Bafut into the former Menchum valley. This is about 2,000 feet above sea level. (Ngwa,1962:10).

The boundaries of the Bamenda grassfields were not static during the colonial era. Under the British administration, the boundaries underwent successive modulation or adjustments. These modifications were made principally to ensure good administration. On 15 August 1920, the Bagam area was handed over to the French Cameroons. On 1 January 1924, the Kaka-Ntem area which was formerly administered under the Gashaka Division of the Yola

Province of Nigeria was transferred to the Bamenda grasslands. In return for this lost territory, Captain Pollock, the British Administrator of Bamenda, handed over the Kentu District to the Nun Division in November 1926 (National Archives Buea, (NAB) File No. Ag 251, Annual Reports for Bamenda Division, 1920, 1924, 1926; Gardinier, 1967:527-528; Ngoh, 2001:9).

## Map 1: A Section of the Bamenda Grassfields Locating the Study Area

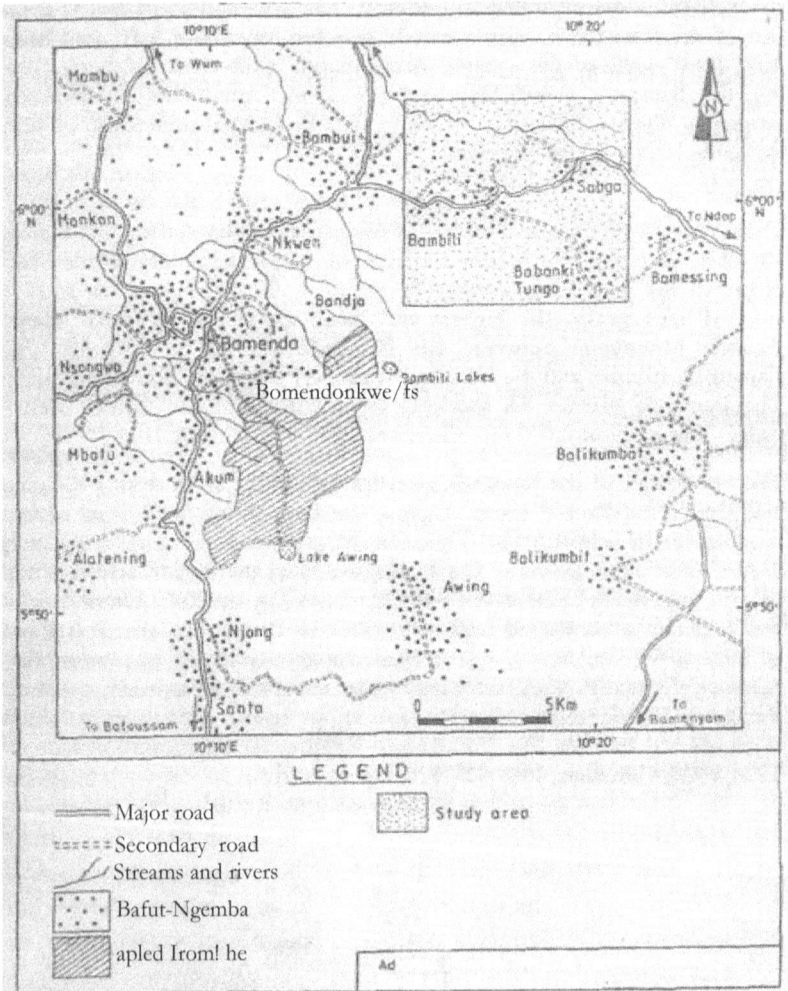

## Locating the Study Area

The villages of Bambili and Babanki-Tungoh formed the group that **made** up the Bafut Native Authority Area of the Bamenda Division of the Cameroons Province in the 1920s (Hawkesworth, 1934). These village-group units lived in the fertile valley basin encompassed on the North by the Kom Mountains and hill ranges; on the West by the distant Meta, Ngie and Ngonu mountains and hill ranges; on the East by the Tingeh hill range and in the South by the escarpment on which the Bamenda station is perched. Bambili is situated on the lower hill-slope of the area and form a small village about 15 kilometres from Bamenda. It shares boundary with Bambui to the Northwest; Babanki-Tungoh to the Southeast and Nkwen to the West. It forms part of Tubah Sub Division of Mezam Division. Babanki-Tungoh is found in the valleys surrounded by hill ranges on the Northern part of the Bambutous Mountains and stretches down to a portion of the Noun plain. It shares common boundaries with Bambili to the North; Bamessi to the East, Sabga to the North East and Balikumbat to the South. (Map 2).

## Historical Background of Bambili and Babanki-tungoh

Bambili and Babanki-Tungoh belong to the Tikar ethnic group and speak the semi-Bantu language (for more on the Bantus read Philip Curtin et. al. 198425-30; Murdock, 1959:46-50 Chilver and Kaberry, 1967:1). Several versions have been advanced, which deal with the historical origins of these two communities. The first account was given by the Fon of Bambili in 1926 and according co this version the Bambili left Ndobo with other Tikar groups like the Bafut. They went directly to their present site passing between Babungo and Bambalang in the Ndop plain. (Hawkesworth,1926; David Shomboin, Personal Communication, December 1999). The name Bambili was derived from Mbili, meaning to sleep. Hawkesworth corroborates these views and maintains that the Mbili met an aboriginal stock in their current abode known as the Nchotilcm. The origin of the Nchotilem has remained a moot question. A conflict developed between the host and the new comers. This stemmed from the fact that Nchitilem wanted to control the dynasty, while the

65

## Map 2: The Babanki-tungo-bambili Boundary Dispute

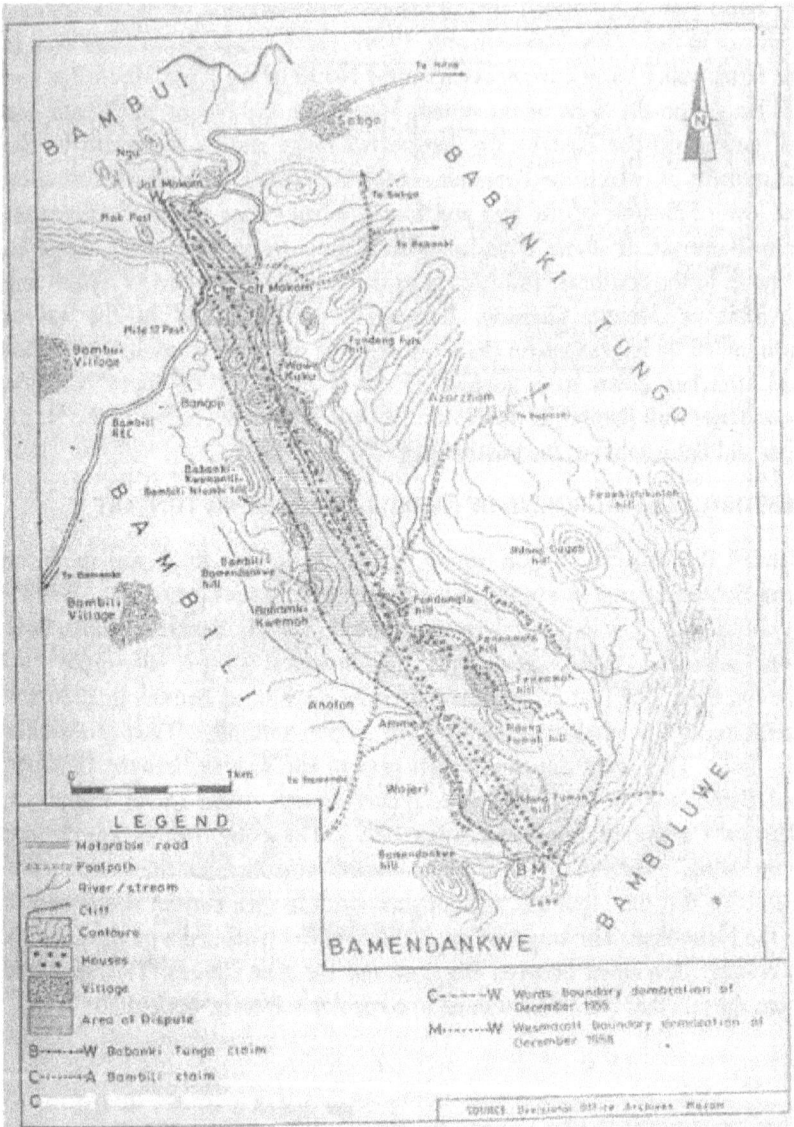

Mbili wanted to maintain their sovereign authority with Ishaten at the head (Hawkesworth, 1926). A compromise was stroke or arrived at between the two factions with Nchotilem condescending to become part of the Mbili dynasty.

Babanki, also called and spelled differently as Babanki-Tungoh (Tungaw, Tungo, and Kidjem-Ketinguh) derived its name from gigantic pillars of rock some hundreds of feet in height that tower on each site of the village. According to their oral tradition they are an off-shoot of Big-Babanki. They broke away from Big-Babanki because of problems that arose in the royal family. It should be noted that the two Babankis left Ndobo together and settled in the present site of Big-Babanki. They co-existed in peace until a disagreement erupted between them on whether to celebrate the annual cultural festival, Kabenkendong or not. This cultural feast coincided with the death of a prince, who just died as the festival was about to begin. This resulted in a split of the people and their migration.

Other sources also maintained that after the dispute in Big-Babanki, the leaders came to Bambili and begged for land on which to settle. This land was given not only by Bambili alone but was contributed by Bamessi and Bandja (Hook, 1934; Bawden and Lagdale, 1962:1-2). Whatever the case, the Bambili and Babanki-Tungoh never arrived at their respective places at the same time. The information elicited from informants in the field hold that the Bambili were the first to arrive in this region (Pa Boleng, Personal Communication, October 2000). However, when land was given to the Babanki-Tungoh there was peaceful co-existence before relations became strained in the second half of the twentieth century, over their common boundary. In examining the causes of the boundary conflict it will be instructive to note that issues extraneous to the border conflict actually accentuated the boundary conflict.

**Contending Issues**
The causes of the boundary dispute between Bambili and Babanki-Tungoh are many and varied. They can be appreciated under the following rubrics: political, economic, social and psychological domains.

Politically, the two neighbours have always shown tendencies of expansionism. At one time or the other, these two villages attempted, although without much success, to subjugate their neighbours. For instance, the Bambili had boundary disputes with Nkwen over Ta'ana, Bambui and Babanki-Tungoh over their common border. Babanki-Tungoh on the other hand, had boundary misunderstanding with Bamessing, Bali-Kumbat and Bambili and this is because of their settlement patterns which make it imperative for them to have problems with their boundary. A case in point is Bambili which is hemmed in, and this hemming is further complicated by the fact that the land at her disposal is scarce in relation to their ever growing population. The scarcity of land experienced by the Bambili can be attributed to government policies in the area since the 1960s. Large parcels of land were appropriated for government projects. For instance, the Cameroon College of Arts, Science and Technology (CCAST) which was opened in 1963 took considerable hectares of arable land from the Bambili. As if that was not enough harm, it was not long afterwards that the Ecole Normale Superieur Annex (ENS)-Bambili; the Regional School of Agriculture; the School of Health Sciences Annex, Bambili (CUSS) and the Gendarmerie Brigade were opened. All these projects took up large chunks of land in an area which already experiences acute arable land scarcity. A ready way out of this parlous situation was for the Bambili to attempt to expand at the expense of their neighbours. More to this, the need to expand is explained in the ever growing population as well as the ever ambition of empire building in the sub region.

Conversely, Babanki-Tungoh is not also found in a very comfortable situation. It is situated on the rocky and narrow end of the Ndop Plain. At the initial time of settlement the first hamlet was located in the valley, which often was enough to sustain the small population thus not necessitated an outward expansion. As time evolves there was the need to expand because of the-growing population and the need for fertile land. In an attempt to expand and annex their respective neighbours, because of an increase in population, the Bambili and Babanki-Tungoh clashed on their common border leading to the boundary conflict. Nonetheless, some informants argue that the need for self-defence either from Bambili or Babanki-Tungoh, and not expansion, led to the boundary conflict (Pa Robert; Pa Jerry and Joseph Buteh, Personal Communication, 20 December 2001).

Furthermore, boundary misunderstandings are not a new phenomenon in this region. In the nineteen century, Bambili and Balikumbat went to war. The causes of that war included, amongst others, the expansionist proclivities of Balikumbat and the misunderstanding over their boundary. During the war, Babanki-Tungoh reached an entente with the Balikumbat and gave them their full military co-operation. The result was that Bambili was defeated. The agreement that ended this war was to impose very harsh terms on the Bambili. These terms included: Bambili was to be vassalage to Balikumbat until the payment of indemnities was completed. This is just an illustration to show that the Bambili - Babanki-Tungoh boundary conflict is a continuum in the sub region.

Another factor which is accountable for this perennial conflict in our area of study is the unrestricted or uncontrolled circulation of guns. The Cameroon Law requires that one obtains a license to be able to possess a gun. With the advent of sophisticated guns, killings have increased by leaps and bounds. This new phenomenon became noticeable within the last two decades of the twentieth century. Hitherto, the combatants had relied on sticks, stones, knives and Dane guns as war implements. With the new situation, killings have become rampant and destruction immense. In a confidential note of 1978, from the Commissioner of Police, Tubah to Divisional Officer, Mezam, it was noted that:

> Information worthy of trust revealed to service agent the Kwifon, the highest secret traditional society in Bambui have [sic] privately instructed all men in Bambui to possess dane guns in preparation for a war against Funge people at any moment from now....(Confidential note, Ref. No. 0212/CF/ 11/B/29/S.12/744 of 3 August 1978).

From the above, certain issues can be deduced. First, that the arms circulation indirectly affects Bambili and Babanki-Tungoh boundary relations. This is so because the geo-political locations of Bambili and Bambui make their boundaries fluid. The fluidity of the boundary implies that what affects Bambui is sure also to affect

Bambili indirectly and/or directly. Secondly, it might be true that without the arms, the violence between Bambili and the Babanki-Tungoh communities would still have arisen. Yet, it is equally true to say that the utilisation of such weapons have accentuated the amount of destruction and casualties.

Another political cause of the boundary conflict is the laxity of the civil administration to competently handle the situation between Bambili and Babanki-Tungoh. The British colonial administration attempted defining and demarcating this boundary. This attempt led to a thaw in the Bambili and Babanki-Tungoh relations. But between c. 1955 and 1995 several complaints were brought before the court. What is more about these complaints is the fact that, court injunctions were contravened by both villages. When this happened effective sanctions were not taken against the defaulting community by the administration. This showed how laxed the administration was. To make the point of the laxity of administration more lucid, the two villages reached an entente on 25 July 1973 (Confidential file No. 0004 of Provincial Archives, Bamenda). Unfortunately, the understanding was violated by the Babanki without any serious reprimand. This certainly gave the impression that the agreement was not considered serious even by the government.

In a related vein, the activities of Abotus, one of the most educated elites in Bambili (Minister in-charge of Special Duties at the Presidency and a member of the CPDM Central Committee) was seen as championing the Bambili course in this conflict. In a confidential release, Abutos (pseudonym) closest associate revealed that Abotus armed the Bambili people with automatic rifles to "crush" the Babanki-Tungoh people "next time" (Beatrice Ngam Ajouh; Pa Akunli, Personal Communication, 10, 11, September 1999).

Economically, the contiguous boundary area between the belligerent parties is extremely fertile. Consequently, the bulk of the farming is carried out in this disputed piece of territory. Farmers have testified to the fact that the bulk of vegetables supplied to the Bamenda metropolis emanates from here. The plausible deduction here is that the entire political economy of this area is sustained largely by the disputed region. To show how the economic factor is very important in the boundary dispute, a confidential release of 15 November 1971 from the Prime Minister's office stated: "It is desirable for the Babanki people to have a market for their potatoes about this area, and so a piece of land should be sliced from the Bambili land on this area and allocated to Babanki-Tungoh for this purpose" (Confidential Note Ref. No. PM 398/T/117 of 15 November 1971). This communiqué points to the fact that economic imperatives account for the boundary dissension. This is more compounded by the fact that, the Bambili were not allowed their land to be sliced and given to Babanki-Tungoh.

The economic imperatives were complicated by the fact that this area is also used for cattle grazing. The Fulani, who arrived this region at the end of the 19th century preferred *to* graze their cattle in the higher slopes free from disease-bearing insects. While the Fulani used this portion of land as pasturage, the villagers used it for the cultivation of crops. A corollary of the above situation was that there was a lot of pressure on the limited land. The scarcity of both grazing and arable land has invariably antagonised the two neighbours. To elucidate the point further, an official cattle market was opened at Sabga (Babanki-Tungoh) by the British colonial administration and the buying of cattle elsewhere in the region other than in the cattle market was strictly prohibited (Annual Reports for Bamenda Division, 1946, 1947 and 1948).

Above all, the fact that this piece of land was used both for farming and as pasturage by the Fulani herdsmen puts a lot of pressure on the land. It would, however, be realised that the grazier-farmer conflict which gave a final push to the boundary conflict stemmed, in the main, from the co-existence of two different patterns of land exploitation. In other words, land use and land holding were not often harmonised.

## The Disputed Area: The Question of Ownership

The boundary conflict between Bambili and Babanki-Tungoh flared up in the 1950s because of a fertile piece of land found between these two villages. In the 1990s, the claims took a different dimension - warfare, causing enormous damages to both villages. This large tract of land is found on top of Sabga hill. On the high ground adjacent to Bambili the land is purely grazing land. It then drops into a valley. This valley is very fertile and it is extensively farmed and built over by the people of Babanki-Tungoh, found on the edge of the Ndop plain. (See map 111)

According to informants, the Bambili people arrived in this area prior to the Babanki-Tungoh people and the highland now in dispute was "no man's land". Both parties were probably using it for hunting (Pa Joseph Buteh, Mike Tune, Personal Communication 23, 26, 28 August 1998; 7 September 1999,). From the mid-20th century the two villages have made claims and counter claims over this land. The question is who owns the land under dispute? If we take into consideration the fact that the Bambili people first arrived in the disputed area, we could as well accept the fact that the disputed land belongs to Bambili. But the situation is bound to be different when we consider who first made a claim over the area in dispute and who is in effective occupation. In as much as the Babanki-Tungoh people have built and are farming on the land, one is tempted to conclude that the land belongs to them. However, for a better understanding of the history of the conflict it is imperative to look at land ownership on the eve of colonisation.

Before colonisation, land was one of the most important resources for the formation of states in the Bamenda grass fields. Even within the states themselves, the ruling authorities struggled over resources of the land. Accordingly, land was important for agriculture, hunting, fishing settlements, crafts and manufacturing amongst others. For these reasons, the land tenure system evolved to be fundamentally communal land and was placed under the household lineage or clan heads. Each family as a constituent of a lineage had the right to land; ownership was transferred to the off springs on inscriptive basis. This took place when the male offspring was getting married and needed land for settlement. In this case therefore, land constituted the basic form of property, status and prestige in the society (Che-Mfombong, 1982:89; Drummond-Hay, 1926).

However, the development of a monarchical system of government and social stratification transformed the basis of land ownership to include other forms of private ownership. In this case, land existed either individually or collectively. Nonetheless, the communal ownership dominated, and all land was, in principle, under the control of the Fon who administered it through their deputies like the quarter wards or village heads, lineage heads and sub-fons. Local laws and customs were put in place prohibiting the sale or pledge of land, but which facilitated its easy transfer from one noble to another. Under this arrangement, the right to perform sacrifices to a local god or other ancestors was also transferred. Only these "nobles" could own large tracts of land or be designated to do the transfers. Similarly, land could be distributed to non lineage members but only after having considered the interest of the immediate lineage and dependants. In the same way, settlement on any land within a polity by an outsider was only permitted by the Fon through his administrative officials.

The advent of the British colonial administration in 1916 saw the introduction of certificate of occupancy. This meant that when the Fon at all possessed land he could lease it out for a period of ninety-nine rears to his subjects or tenants. But it should be borne in mind that this did confer titles because though land was leased to the individual, the Fon remained the "Lord manor". According to Ordinance No. 74-1 of 6th July 1974, the certificate of occupancy was abolished and following Decree No. 76/165/27 of April 1976, new conditions were established for obtaining the land certificate. Article one of the Decrees stipulates that land certificate shall be the only authentic document of real property rights(Wilson, 1981:98). This means that without this document it was difficult to claim land.

With regard to Bambili and Babanki-Tungoh, they have been claiming the piece of land on their border, yet none of them could show any document proving their claims. Instead, the Bambili point to Lake Bambili as their ancestral home. They also maintain that every year libations are performed in the lake to appease the ancestors and to have a good harvest during the farming season. The Babanki-Tungoh also argued that the lake is theirs and the entire piece of land. What is more is the fact that both villages do not possess a land certificate or the defunct certificate of occupancy. On the backdrop of this, it is fair and within the common sense for us to contend that the land belongs to the "first comers" which is Bambili. Evidence garnered from the field also elicit that it was Bambili who gave land to the Babanki-Tungoh.

The failure of Bambili and Babanki-Tungoh to produce a land certificate might "be attributed to their ignorance or their firm knowledge on African concept of land ownership. Perhaps, the administration could have taken off time to orientate both parties and use this practical logic and commonsense, but the administrators: always rushed to the disputed area for inspection. A case in point was the Divisional Officer, Bamenda Central Sub Division, Oben Peter Ashu, who on 26 June 1975, inspected the disputed area and issued letter No. ABA 23/681 of 18 September 1975. In that letter, he gave directives to Ardo Jacky of Sabga, Babanki-Tungoh and the farmers of Chuku on what should be done before farming on the area (Confidential letter from the Fon of Babanki-Tungoh to Divisional Officer, Tubah, 9 October 1995). That was as far as he could go.

What is important to note is the issue of obtaining a land certificate which was not stressed by Ashu in his bit of demands to the people neither did he employ the traditional method of ascertaining the ownership of land. The land became national land. This had been echoed by Honourable S.N. Kindo, an educated elite of Bambili; when he said: "it is the role of the government to make the best use of land they have and not to allow it stand wasted (Minutes of the Traditional Council meeting with Hon. Mukong and 1 Ion. Kindo on 16 January 1972 in the chiefs palace in Babanki-Tungoh to find out a peaceful solution to the Babanki-Tungoh/Bambili boundary dispute page, 2.). Kindo's statement stressed the fact that since neither Bambili nor Babanki-Tungoh possessed the land certificate, the disputed land should not be allowed to waste, and instead, the government should take good care of it.

The arguable question in the land debate is: who should produce the certificate? Is it the individual or the community? If it is the community, could it be possible for the whole community to possess one certificate? The role of the Fon becomes very important. He is, according to what existed before colonisation, the "Lord Manor" and leases out land to his subjects. This is evident in a letter written by the chief of Babanki-Tungoh on 29 June 1973, addressed to the Assistant Cattle Control Officer, Bafut Area Council. In that letter the Fon among other things said: "This is to certify that I the Fon of Babanki-Tungoh, have [sic] given a plot to Mr. Joseph Mbuate —

Tangem nearest to Align ale at the lake. He is going to do farming there and to make a license round the farming plot. So I hereby wish to inform you and your office so as to let you know (Fon of Babanki-Tungoh to the Assistant Cattle Control Officer, Bafut Area Council, 29 June 1973). With this, it *is* clear that the Fon owns the land and leases or distributed it to his subjects. But according to Articles 9-10 of Decree No. 76/165 of April 1976 establishing conditions of obtaining land certificate, the Fon do not own any inch of village land they are merely custodians. In the event of a border conflict, it is logical that his subjects will defend the boundary, essentially, because the Fon is looked up as the "hope" of the community. However, since 1950s the boundary conflict between these two communities has manifested itself in various ways.

### Manifestation of the Conflict C. 1950-1995

Boundary conflict within the study area has manifested itself in three principal ways: from c. 1950 to 1958 it was mainly in the form of law suits filed by the contestants; from 1958 to 1973 it led to the signing if Babanki-Tungoh and Bambili "entente." This second period can be called the period of "thaw" in the boundary manifestation. The last period was from 1973 to 1995, a period characterised by skirmishes, threat, suspicion and outright warfare. It ended in 1995 with yet another law suit.

### The Period of Court Rulings, C. 1950s-1958

This period kept the colonial administration busy. It began with the Bambili people bringing a suit against the Babanki-Tungoh people in the Bafut Native Court Civil Suit No. 23/53. As already mentioned, this claim was made over a piece of land bordering the two communities. The court judgment of 11 December 1953 situated the boundary on the hills, on the West side of the outlet of the lake and valley. The court granted Bambili part of the land which the Bambili had claimed. This land stretched from the German boundary of Babanki-Tungoh with Mendankwe at "Kukets" to the hills west of the lake and valley. The Bambili were not, however, satisfied with the decision. They claimed that it was unjust. As a result of this, they appealed and in the judgment of 15 July 1955, the Appeal Court shifted the line to the high grazing land near to the escarpment beyond, which is Bambili village. Yet, they were still not satisfied and called for a review by the Colonial District Officer. On 8 September, 1956 the Assistant Divisional Officer, Ward, rendered his review judgment. And according to him, the boundary began:

At the very high peak at the boundary with Bambulue into the Twentueng stream. It will follow streams in the same general direction until it reaches the cattle tract near markets ruga. There a cairn will be erected and the boundary will move in a straight line to the raffia bush on the stream that comes across the main road just beyond mile 13. (The Native Courts Ordinance *Cap.* 142, laws of Nigeria cited in the Review Jurisdiction of the Resident, Bamenda holden at Bafut, Review No. 84/56,File No. 365 (569), 15 May 1959). Wards review judgment came close to giving Bambili most of their claims.

He went on to add:

Anybody from either village who now finds himself on land not owned by his own people will have the choice of moving to his own village land or staying where he is and paying tax to the new village. If he chooses to do the latter he will be permitted to stay and farm. Persons who choose to move must do so before 1 January 1957. This will give them time to harvest their crops. (The Native Courts Ordinance Op. 142, laws of Nigeria cited in the Review Jurisdiction of the Resident, Bamenda holden at Bafut, Review No. 84/56, File No. 365 (569), 15 May 1959)

What pushed Ward to arrive at this was that he doubted whether the boundary between Bambili and Babanki-Tungoh had ever been defined let alone demarcated. His qualms were made clearest when he said:

In my opinion correctly, I do not think that the boundary had ever been defined between the parties. It is my opinion that the decisions of the Court of first Instance and the Court of Appeal were on more than many attempts to arbitrate. They both failed because they chose an unsuitable and artificial line. It is my intention to create a more suitable natural boundary (Native Court Ordinance Cap. 142, Review No. 84/56, File NO. 365 (569), 15 May 1959).

In an attempt to "create a more suitable natural boundary" Ward aroused the, disenchantment of Babanki-Tungoh people. It was a result of this discontent that the Babanki-Tungoh demanded for a review. That review was rendered on 15 May 1958 by A.B. Westmacott, colonial resident in Bamenda According to ' his judgment in review No. 84/56 in File No. 361 (569) Ward's decision was lopsided since he maintained that many Babanki-Tungoh people were affected and no Bambili man was even required to make a choice. A.B. Westmacott, after having inspected the land for three days decided that Babanki-Tungoh should remain in possession of the land which they now occupy but that all the grazing land on the Bambili side which [was] now occupied – with the exception of three Babanki-Tungoh and several Fulani rugas should be confirmed as belonging to Bambili. Starting from Bambili Lake, the boundary will be as decided by the Appeal Court until it approaches the foot path running from Babanki-Tungoh to Bamenda. It will then bear almost due north from this point along the grassy spur until it reaches a rocky outcrop on the steep escarpment defining the valley. It will run along the edge of this escarpment until the cliff-like feature ends and the land becomes rolling clown land. The boundary will then follow the line as defined by cairns until it reaches the main Bamenda-Kumbo-Nkambe Road (Ring Road) at the sharp corner just beyond mile post 13. (NAB, File No. 385)

The Westmacott decision has remained on the map. What was required was that the decision on the map be utilised for the demarcation of the disputed area. However, when this decision was arrived at, on 15 May 1958, the two villages reacted differently to it. The map was drawn on 30 May 1958, by J.M. Mbafor who surveyed the land in accordance with the decision of delimitation (Minutes of a Traditional Council Meeting with lion. Mukong and Hon. Kindo at the Fon's Palace in Babanki-Tungoh, signed by the chairman of Babanki-Tungoh traditional Council, 16 January 1972).

## The 1958-1973 Period

The Bambili people, it was reported, were not satisfied with the above decision of Westmacott and in April 1959, the Fon of Bambili petitioned in Civil Suit No. 23/53 against the decision to the Government of the Southern Cameroons. On 8 July 1959, the

Deputy Commissioner of the Southern Cameroons, J.A.A Tamkoh, replied to the petition in the following words "I am directed to refer to your petition of April 1959, and to inform you that it is regretted that Government cannot interfere with the judgment of resident" Q.A.A. Tamkoh to the Fon of Bambili, Letter No. 362-569/T/19 of 9 July 1959). Babanki-Tungoh people were not satisfied with the Westmacott decision neither. As a result of this, they paid the sum of 138.400 FCFA in July 1967 as deposited for an appeal against part of the boundary marked by the 1958 decision. Unfortunately, this appeal was never heard.

However, on 25 July, 1973, both villages signed an agreement acknowledging and accepting the Westmacott decision as the only authentic document. This was following attempted demarcations by Area Surveyor and Lands Officer, Kay Simo, on 16 November 1971 and the Divisional Officer for Bamenda Central, D.N.N. Pufong on 8 March 1972. It was hoped that the decision would put an end to the long standing boundary dispute between the two communities. The entente was signed by the Fons of Babanki-Tungoh and Bambili for their communities. This "understanding" was witnessed by the Cameroon Representative, Ngonge Sone; B.N. Mukong for Babanki-Tungoh; S-N. Kindo for Bambili and several land and survey officers."(A copy of the Bambih/Babanki-Tungoh entente terms reached between the respective Fons on 25 July 1973, in the presence of a Cameroon administrative witnesses; Ngonge Sone, S.N. Kindo and B.N. Mukong, witnesses for Bambili and Babanki-Tungoh). As a result of the entente, peace reigned in the sub-region, albeit in the midst of tears, threats and scepticism. Every possible effort was made by the administration of the Bamenda Division to provide a peaceful solution to the problem. Farming activities were authorised by the Farmer Grazier Department and all persons who were authorised to retain their farms in this area were required to obtain farming permits from the farmer/grazier branch in regularisation of the land they occupied in the area. (For more on the Grazier/Farmer problem see, Report on the Cameroon Under United Kingdom Trusteeship for the year 1949, 1950, 87; Report on the Cameroons Under United Kingdom Trusteeship for the year 1948, 1949, 280).

## The Peace and War Decades, 1973-1995

Though some degree of peace reigned for more than a decade after the Westmacott decision and the 1973 accord, the boundary conflict manifestation took a different dimension and magnitude in the early 1990s. This was because the early 1990s witnessed the stockpile of weapons, the rising aspirations of the indigenes and their rulers to expand and annex the piece of land under dispute, the involvement of politicians and the training of local militia men. These factors increased the amount of threat, tensions and fears amongst the indigenes of both villages which culminated in open armed clashes in 1991, 1993 and 1995.

It is germane to note that before the 1991 outbreak of war, the 1973 peace-accord had earlier been violated. On 1 August 1981, the Fon of Bambili reported to the Civil Administration that the Babanki-Tungoh people were still continuing their activities in the disputed area. In response, on 17 April 1986, the District Officer of Tubah reported to the Divisional Officer for Mezam and called it a "provocative trespass" into Bambili land by the Babanki-Tungoh people. In his reply, the Divisional Officer for Mezam stated that he had convoked the "ring leaders" of the aggressive groups to his office rot-interrogation and cautioning. The provocation, nonetheless, continued uninterrupted, and on 24 May 1991, the Bambili people went to the disputed area and started farming. The Babanki-Tungoh community replied by attacking Bambili on 25 May 1991. This led to the outbreak of the first Babanki-Tungoh/Bambili war.

From the above account it is obvious that the violation of the agreement between the two communities facilitated the escalation of the armed conflict. The terms of the agreement had explained that any person encroaching on the disputed area would "lie penalised by the administration". This was not the case. The only thing that was done to the trespassers was that the "ring leaders" were called and cautioned by the District Officer. During this confrontation, property and lives were destroyed and several families were rendered homeless. When the dust finally settled on the issue, the Administration of Tubah, under the District Officer, Martin Jum, and the Mezam Divisional Administration under the Senior Divisional Officer, Bell Luc Rene, set up an administrative commission to investigate and resolve the .problem.

The 1991 commission began by attempting to retrace the boundary to satisfy both parties. In spite of all the painstaking efforts to resolve the dispute, the inhabitants of Babanki-Tungoh and Bambili violated one of the agreed terms of the commission — there was to be no farming around the disputed area. The inhabitants of both villages farmed on disputed area, crops and eucalyptus trees were planted and fences were built around the farms. Both parties attempted to expand their farms and, by so doing, transgressed beyond the boundary line. The Babanki-Tungoh people were also accused on grounds that they sounded war trumpets; chanted war songs and threatened Bambili women on their farms around the disputed area. The Bambili people on their part were blamed for having trained fighters and destroyed crops in the farms owned by Babanki-Tuhgoh people, and blocked the Bamenda-Ndop-Kumbo road as well as the Bambili-Mbingo highway. All these snowballed into another war, in 1993.

On 23 January 1993, there were fresh provocations. The Babanki-Tungoh people asserted that the Bambili indigenes came up to their side of the boundary and embarked on crop destruction, "chopped" down a young eucalyptus forest and set a Babanki-Tungoh man's compound on fire. This act was immediately reported to the administration by the Babanki elites who claimed there was evidence to show that it was the Bambili people who were responsible for the destruction. (Report written by Mr. Jum, District Officer for Tubah on the Babanki-Tungoh/Bambili War of 1991, 10 August 1991).

According to the administration, the Bambili people should have been arrested in the very act of destruction. On 26 January 1993, Bambili people blocked the Bamenda to Ndop and Bamenda Bandja-Babanki-Tungoh highways and attacked Babanki-Tungoh. This strategy according to Bambili people was because most of the Babanki people had gone to Big Babanki for the annual traditional festival, Kabenkendong. The Babanki-Tungoh people rushed back and confronted the Bambili. Before the Bambili could launch an assault the Babanki-Tungoh people had burnt down some houses and several people were wounded.

The Senior Divisional Officer for Mezam, Samuel Sufo, went to the battle on 27 January 1993, and attempted to appease the belligerents. The warring factions retreated but fighting resumed the next day and continued for more than a week before the administration brought in Gendarmes. Six "ring leaders" were arrested from Babanki-Tungoh and detained in the Gendarmerie Brigade for having instigated the fighting (Chumboin Pius, Personal Communication 25 August 1999,). It is important to note that the war broke out when the 1991 commission set up by the Administration was still at work in an attempt to find solutions to the dispute.

When the war abetted, the Divisional Officer for Tubah inspected the area and found out that the boundary had been violated by both sides. To further demarcate the boundary he planted pillars and pegs in the absence of the two pillars involved, holding that they could protest after he must have finished the job. He ignored the 1958 Westmacott decision, an act which was detested by both parties. A sub-technical commission was formed in 1994 charged with special functions of settling the boundary dispute in a way acceptable to all the factions. The sub technical commission, as a matter of fact, made futile- efforts to settle the boundary feud. Yet, activities still went on unabated in the dispute area against the terms of the commission. The end-result was the war of 1995.

The Bambili/Babanki Tungoh war of 1995 broke out fundamentally because the Bambili and the Babanki-Tungoh violated the "new" boundary. Secondly, the Divisional Officer for Tubah attempted to demarcate the boundary without the presence of the two parties involved. Thirdly, the 1994 sub technical commission's torpid attitude towards the demarcation of the boundary was very pivotal. This war went on for three days and it was fought with renewed ferocity by both belligerents until the forces of law and order intervened and stopped it. The prompt intervention of the forces of law and order never gave breathing space for any "terms" to be deliberated upon. When the Senior Divisional Officer for Mezam, Samuel Sufo, attempted another demarcation the Babanki-Tungoh people "dragged" him to the Bamenda High Court on 3 July 1995. They claimed that he attempted to impose a boundary on them without making reference to the Westmacott boundary.

## An Appraisal

The foregoing analysis reveals that various attempts were made aimed at resolving the Bambili and Babanki-Tungoh boundary conflict. These attempts included meetings convened by the civil administration, traditional and educational elite; the formation of commissions, and attempted demarcations. Although the endeavour to demarcate the boundary in 1971 and 1972, all in an attempt to resolve the boundary conflict failed, it should be noted that they were genuine attempts at bringing about a peaceful resolution of the conflict. Despite these attempts, a lasting and acceptable solution to the protracted boundary crisis has eluded every party involved. This unfortunate situation can be ascribed to the following reasons:

> First of all, the two communities have refused to cooperate in the search for lasting peace. On 16 November1971, the attempt to demarcate the boundary failed principally because of the intransigence of the Babanki-Tungoh. This point was graphically portrayed by Area surveyor and Lands officer, Kay Simo, on 18 November 1971. Simo's report revealed that the demarcation attempt failed because of the attitude of the Babanki-Tungoh people who failed to see reasons for the demarcation attempt. The Area Surveyor and Land Officer and the other administrators used their initiatives to meet the Fon of Babanki-Tungoh to cooperate in the search for a solution. His position as well as those of his compatriots has been vacillating when it comes to putting into practice decisions reached. The "foot-dragging" attitude adopted by the Babanki has delayed the peace process. Their attitude stemmed from the fact that "they had paid the usual land Tribunal deposit and had expected that the Tribunal should go into the matter-which they rejected the Westmacott Administrative boundary, which is now being imposed on them". (Confidential letter from the Director of Lands and Surveys, West Cameroon, A.L. Anyangwe, to the Secretary General, Secretariat of State for the Interior, Buea, 9 December 1971).

Another attempt to bring to an end the boundary conflict failed because the Babanki-Tungoh people failed to honour an invitation by the Divisional Officer of Bamenda Central Sub-Division, D.N.N.

Pufong. On 8 March 1972, Pufong regretted the situation and in his letter to the Area Surveyor and Lands Officer said:

> Unfortunately the chief of Babanki-Tungoh and his councillors failed to turn up, although they actually received my invitation. After a short discussion the two parliamentarians (Hon. B.N. Mukong and S.N, Kindo), the Fon of Bambili and his councillors agreed that the Area Surveyor should carry on the erection of the pillars according to the Westmacott decision and if the Babanki-Tungoh Community felt dissatisfied they were free to petition to the Government.... (Divisional Officer, D.N.N. Pufong to the Area Survey and Lands Officer, 8 March 1972).

From the above it can be concluded at this juncture that the failure of the Babanki — Tungoh people to cooperate in resolving the crisis made the efforts towards a peaceful solution ineffective. Closely related to the above fact, is the issue that the injunction order No. 290.2/C.18.162 of January 1991 was, on the other hand, also violated by the Bambili. This was on 7 May 1991 when the Bambili started farming in the disputed area. With this action, it became difficult to arrive at a peaceful solution to the boundary conflict between the two communities in question.

Another factor that has stood in the way of a peaceful resolution of the conflict is the inherent determination of these communities to seek revenge. In a letter, Ref. No. E2901.2/165/302, from the Sub Divisional Officer, Tubah, Kamga, to the Divisional Officer, Mezam on 16 November 1995, Kamga remarked:

> It is clear that peace is a far away cry between the two communities [Bambili and Babanki - Tungoh]. The two are full of reciprocal hatreds at all. The solution doesn't lie in confrontation. They don't take into consideration the serious consequences of proceeding conflicts. One even wonders if it is for this strip of land at the summit of the hill that they are fighting so much for, it seems to me that the real problem should be the rivalry between the two neighbours and as long as this sentiment of hatred persists, the risk of confrontation shall remain a permanent phenomenon (Translation is mine). This meant that the two neighbouring communities were not prepared to "bury the hatchet."

Furthermore, there have been many groups and individuals involved in the attempts to resolve the conflict. For instance, the colonial administration, civil administration; the Bafut chiefs; Traditional councils; and educated elites have been involved in their turns since the inception of the conflict. What is more, is the fact that these groups failed to build from past efforts preferring instead to adopt new approaches each time they intervened. Thus, these independent approaches and varying resolutions have helped to confuse the parties concerned, and negatively affected the peace process. The genuine interpretation and implementation of the Westmacott decision was not successful. The two communities though did not initially believe in the decision saw in it a temporary relief to hang on. Consequently, when a map was drawn, it was opposed by the Babanki-Tungoh, on the grounds that it was different from that which was approved by Westmacott. For this and several other reasons the Babanki — Tungoh refused to cooperate.

What is more, the surveyors charged with the demarcation were not the "local" surveyors agreed upon in the 1973 agreement. These surveyors displayed ignorance on the field with regard to identifying the bearing on the ground as they were on the map. In a petition against the demarcation by the Babanki -Tungoh to the Senior Divisional Officer, the ignorance of the "Yaounde experts" was put in the following words:

We decided to give the said experts a chance and follow them to the lake where the Westmacott decision of 1958, page two, paragraph five, line six, clearly stated where the boundary starts from but the experts and the SDO's party went parallel to and far beyond the lake to take their bearing and from there decided, rather embarrassingly into Kedjom Tinguh (Babanki-Tungoh) where people lived long before the Westmacott decision of 1958. (Chairman of Babanki-Tungoh, Personal, Communication, 14 December 2000).

The above citation portrayed that the surveyors from Yaounde knew little or nothing about the disputed site. To buttress the point further, the surveyor, B.N. Mukong, educated elite of Babanki-Tungoh, in a report to Divisional Officer for Mezam, dated 27 January 1972 explained that:

We were at a loss where to go next from the lake. I observe here that the outlet of the lake and its course did not show the true position on the land. As to the next hill, we gave diverse directions. The scale of the map itself is misleading. After several proposals we decided to go to the nearest Fulani huts... (Ibid.).

The ignorance displayed by the "experts" made any attempt at a peaceful resolution far-fetched. The two quotations above show that the so called technocrats from Yaounde were not conversant with the topography.

The suspicion and scepticism of both parties concerning the objectivity of the civil administration militated against the peaceful resolution of the conflict. Reports from both parties showed that they doubted the honesty of the various Sub-Divisional Officers involved in the matter. This explains why the Senior Divisional Officer for Mezam, Samuel Sufo, convened several peace meetings. He was at one time, accused of favouring the Bambili and at another time the Babanki-Tungoh. It was also because of similar suspicion that the Babanki-Tungoh withdrew their cooperation during the last demarcation exercise in 1995. When matters came to a head, the SDO for Mezam was taken to court to answer charges as to whether he had any powers to change or alter the Westmacott decision which was agreed upon by the two communities.

Furthermore, the two communities have failed to recognise the time-lag Between the Westmacott decision and current attempts at demarcation. This means that within this long period, new developments have taken place in the area under dispute consequently weakening the force of the Westmacott decision, And because of this any attempt to hinge at the Westmacott decision, without taking into effect the changes ended up in futility. The Area. Surveyor and Lands Officer called the attention of the Director of Lands and Surveys Department, Buea on 15 February 1972, and lucidly made the point in the following words:

It must not be forgotten that [the] survey and demarcation of the Bambili and Babanki-Tungo boundary today is based largely on the Westamacott [sic] Decision taken in 1958, and it is not surprising that several changes and developments have taken place (on the ground) over this long period of 14 to 15 years (Area Surveyor and Lands Officer (North West), Bamenda to the Director of Lands and Survey Department, Buea 15 February 1972),

From the foregoing analysis, it is clear that several attempts were made to solve the boundary conflict during the colonial and post-colonial period. These attempts failed for several reasons which have already been mentioned. The Bambili and Babanki-Tungoh have made claims and counter-claims to the land on their border; they have gone to war and several attempts to resolve the perennial conflict have ended up in failure. It is therefore within reason, at this juncture, to suggest some possible solutions. Which if implemented might resolve this boundary conflict once and for all.

## Recommendations

Boundary conflicts are as old as man and there have always been ways and means adopted towards the resolution of boundary conflicts. At times solutions geared towards the resolution of boundary conflicts have failed. It is because attempted solutions to the Bambili and Babanki-Tungoh boundary conflict have failed, that the following section provides some suggestions aimed at resolving the boundary conflict.

In the foregoing analysis, it was realised that two commissions were formed with the aim of resolving the boundary conflict. These commissions failed because of several reasons. However, from the point of view of concrete institution-building, there is perhaps no better evidence than the creation of a boundary commission. This commission should have a legal backing and a good text of application; preferably an act of parliament or presidential decree. The commission should comprise the representatives of the state: Ministers of Defence, Territorial Administration, Justice as well as the Delegate General in Charge of Internal Security, one member nominated by the President, and representatives from the villages concerned (Asiwaju, 1985). Furthermore, the Commission will be charged with the sole responsibility of resolving border conflicts and conflict prevention in the country. It should operate through two technical committees under the Ministry of Territorial Administration.

Besides, it has been evident that attempts have failed because of new topographic developments that have taken place since the Westmacott Decision of 1958. One suggestion to this effect is what Boggs refers to as "simplification of the boundary function". The Bambili and Babanki-Tungo boundary should be retained but its functions should be reduced to allow it to assume more welcoming functions as lines of positive and productive contact. The solution to the Bambili and Babanki-Tungoh boundary conflict might rest in the "simplification of the boundary function". (Boggs, 1940:240-243;). This approach is not a novelty in itself because boundaries else where in Africa have been readjusted to assume more welcoming functions. For instance "in 1904 a particularly tortuous piece of political geometry redefined the Anglo-French frontier in Sokoto (Hargreaves, 1984:25). This was made in order to galvanise the movement of cattle caravans with Niger, Again in 1911 there was an adjustment of the Sierra-Leonean -Liberian border whose main objective was to restore the unity of Luawa chiefdom. From all these, therefore, it is indicative that the Bambili Babanki-Tungoh boundary should undergo some readjustments with the cardinal objective of bringing the two peoples together.

Furthermore, contact *per se* is a double-edged sword. Although contact is necessary for boundary conflict, it can also be highly conducive and volatile for the reduction of boundary conflict. The solution to boundary conflict could lie in increased contact. It is important to note that boundary conflict is further reduced when there is contact between equal status members of Bambili and Babanki-Tungoh. This is possible because the Bambili and Babanki-Tungoh villages are not separated by serious natural features - rivers, mountains, and valleys. Thus, the fluidity of the boundary gives room for contact and, therefore, if the situation is better handled, it will reduce conflict (Hargreaves, 1984:30; Mack, 1963:376). More so, the Border-Landers ought to understand that interaction with the other side is frequently a matter of necessity and even survival. This is especially true with the two neighbouring communities because there is a pronounce level of economic inter-dependence.

Another suggestion that can bring peace between the two warring communities is to determine who owns the disputed land. From the foregoing analysis, it has been very difficult to determine who owns the piece of land because none of the villages is showing convincing evidence that the disputed piece of land is theirs. As a result, the land becomes national land, According to Part II of Ordinance No. 77-1 of 10 January 1977, "National lands shall of right comprise lands which at the date on which the present Ordinance enters into force, are not classed into the public or private property of the state and other public others" (Wilson, 1986: 99). Based on this, the government can transform this land into a national forest. The government can accelerate agricultural activities in the area by opening up an experimentation farm which will be an affiliate to the Regional School of Agriculture in Bambili or Institute for Animal Research (I.R.Z) Bambui. By so doing, the two communities will relent from carrying out acts of aggression in the disputed area. The government could build a school or hospital on the disputed piece of land for the people of both villages,

The government can encourage "Provincialism." This means that the indigenes should have a sense of belonging to a province and therefore defend the pride of the province. If the Cameroon "nation" is a combination of provinces which are made up of clan lineages, it could safely be said that a problem cannot be solve at a macro-level when the micro-level is ignored. In this case, the indigenes of the province are compelled to know and carved out certain objectives geared towards the socio-economic development of their province. For instance, the North West Elite Association and the Chiefs Conference should be overhauled in terms of objectives and structure. Above all, a regional organisation charged with the development of the Babanki-Tungoh and Bambili could be created. The organisation, if formed, could be baptized the Bambili/ Babanki-Tungoh Development Association (B.B.A.T.U.D.A).

This attempt was indeed carried out by the Mexican and United States of American government on their common border. In 1961 the Mexican government working in conjunction with the US government inaugurated the Programa Nacional Fronterizo (PRONAF) which was further replaced in 1967 by the Border Industrial Programme (BIP) (Asiwaju, 1984:244). Although the two governments did not carry out these efforts because of boundary misunderstandings it should be noted, however, that these developmental border programme can help tremendously to reduce the incidence of border conflict hence leading to the development of Bambili and Babanki-Tungoh. An African parallel model to the above is the rural development programme of the Zambian Government astride Zambian boundaries with Malawi with special focus on the Chewa and the Ngoni communities (Phin, 1985:105-125).

Furthermore, the media should be used to educate and orientate the two warring communities. Most of the time the written and audio-visual press has been instruments of revenge and attacks thereby creating a permanent state of instability. Most privately owned newspapers in Cameroon are more interested in headlines that provoke conflicts than those that resolve them. It is generally believed that conflict starts in the mind before it gets on to the battle field; such newspapers whip up war hysteria (Ngwane, 1996:34-35). To those who do not understand the English Language, vernacular programmes could be run on Radio Bamenda on a weekly basis emphasizing the need for a peaceful co-existence. The two communities should have seasoned journalists who will always sensitise their people. With such a network, the media will become more responsible to human development and more contributively towards nation-building.

Another suggestion worth emulating is what has been done elsewhere in Africa where there are lakes or rivers separating countries. These include the Lake Chad Commission created and run by Nigeria, Chad, Niger and Cameroon. These countries had vested interest in this important inland water. There is also the Mano River Union between Sierra Leone and Liberia and the Niger Rivet-Basin Commission connecting Nigeria, Benin, Niger, Mali and Guinea (Conakry). Although these Rivers and Lakes commissions are/were to be created because of boundary conflict *per se*, they understandably reduced the degree of boundary conflict.

This case is more plausible for Bambili and Babanki-Tungoh to burlesque because there is a Lake which is found on their common border. This lake has been claimed by Bambili as their ancestral home as well as Babanki-Tungoh. This means that the lake is symbolically the 'soul' of the two belligerent communities either rightly or wrongly. This is more so, because the two villages pour libations on this lake and equally use the waters for the irrigation of their crops.

Therefore, the lake Bambili/Babanki-Tungoh Commission could be created with the sole function of development strategies. The commission which should consists of members from Bambili and Babanki-Tungoh will be charged with drawing up objectives that can help the two villages see reason in meaningful development rather than always rushing to war and destroying the resources which could help in the development of this zone.

Finally, a pastoral approach could be used to resolve the boundary conflict (Gam, 1997:22-32; Kucher, 1981:1076-1084). This could be done if the differences that exist among the denominations — the Presbyterian, Baptists and Catholics are neutralised. If an effort is made to use this method, the various denominations should take two fundamental points into consideration:

Firstly, they should attempt to go beyond conflict resolution and comprise belief and values that stand as obstacles to non-violent peace-making; secondly, they should keep in mind that their objective is not only to avoid harm or injury but also to organise each community to seek the good of the other by making the adversary a friend. In human relations, it might be difficult but not impossible.

## Conclusion

Boundary conflicts became a thorny issue in the body politics of African states during and after Colonialism. The main factors responsible for these boundary conflicts were political, economic and social. Within the emergent African states, some ethnic groups had boundary misunderstandings with their neighbours. A case in point was the Bambili and Babanki-Tungoh of the North West Province of Cameroon. Available evidence has shown that this conflict was precipitated by social, economic and political factors. It has also shown that the boundary conflict between these two communities was a product of the ever-growing centralised state formation characterised by ambitious, expansionist and hegemonic rulers. Furthermore, based on available evidence gathered from the field the chapter has concluded that the piece of land under dispute belongs to Bambili.

Finally, man remains the architect of his destiny. The long outstanding boundary conflict that has rocked the two communities since the 1950s and has led to enormous costs would have been resolved. Since, naturally, man's activities are teleguided by greed and ambition, the boundary conflict is going on ad nauseam. History has revealed that boundary and/or land disputes have remained a burning issue since time immemorial and the Bambili and Babanki-Tungoh boundary conflict is just a microcosm of what is happening in Africa with regard to boundary conflicts. Attempts at resolving this conflict have failed. This paper has provided some recommendation to the Government and bellicose neighbours, which if implemented will bring an end to this seemingly perennial boundary conflict. The next chapter will turn its focus to the South West Elites Association within the context of the politics of belonging.

# Chapter Five

## Elites, Ethno-regional Competition in Cameroon, 1991-1997: The Case of South West Elites Association (SWELA)

### Introduction

The construction of ethnicity by ethnic elites assumed a wider dimension in most African countries south of the Sahara after 1990. The reasons were many and various, and *inter alia,* included the efforts made by authoritarian regimes to retain power and ethno-regional elites gaining access to the state and its resources. Cameroon was not an exception. This chapter critically explores how the Southwest Elites Association (SWELA) and its historical antecedent fit into ethno-regional politics and the invention of ethnicity in Cameroon. It also attempts to show how the government has used SWELA, and how SWELA, in turn, used the government to achieve its own aims. At both levels the two parties are manipulated.

### General Observations and Objectives

According to Searl (1995), the mind imagines ideas, institutions, and materials, and makes them effective in daily operations. He argues that collective consciousness and compromise can construct certain beliefs that may later become enduring and effective, so much so that, in time, they could be seen as natural. The idea of social identity conforms to and confirms Searl's theory. Social identities, whether manifested in class groupings, gender, or ethnic classifications, are potential targets for conflict and violence. Ethnicity, in particular, plays a significant role in the prevailing crisis of development facing Africa today. In Cameroon, the focus of this chapter, colonial and post-colonial periods produced ethnic groupings, which gave rise to what will be referred to in this chapter as elites, or ethnic elites. The creation of social identities, and giving them substance, has given rise to ethnic regions. In this chapter I defend the position that elites have been at the centre of the effort to manipulate ethnic diversity in Cameroon, a phenomenon begun by the colonial regimes that has been developed by post-colonial elites (political and traditional) for their own self-interested ends. Throughout the course of this manipulation, the regime in power has used ethnic associations to maintain power.

In 1990, many parts of Africa south of the Sahara embraced a new political dynamic. There was an unprecedented drive towards political and economic liberalization, including threats to evict most African dictators, sparked by a general call for democratization and the consequent rebirth of multi-party politics. Political kleptocrats responded by engendering and intensifying the struggle over belonging and forms of exclusion among their citizens. Some were branded "natives," while others were called "strangers", even if they were citizens of the same country. Although this undermined the very notion of national citizenship, which most regimes in Africa had upheld in the early 1960s and 1970s, using unity as a precondition for nation building (Geschiere, 2004 and 2009), these same authoritarian regimes began encouraging conflict between indigenous groups and strangers to remain in power. In Cameroon in particular, the ruling government since 1990, under Paul Biya, has placed additional emphasis on ethnicity, making use of political and traditional elites. This effort was born out of a neo-patrimonialistic and clientelistic system in which appointments were made based on one's relation to the government rather than on merit and ability. In this way, it became fashionable to use ethnic associations to retain the government in power.

The ethnic associations in Cameroon included the Southwest Elite Association (SWELA); the Northwest Elite Association (NOWELA); the elites of the Grand North representing the interests of the three northern provinces of Adamawa, North, and Far North; Essingan, representing the Beti and Bulu heterogeneous groups of the Centre Province; SAWA, representing the interests of the litto-ral people; and LAAKAM of the Bamilekes of the West Province. In some of these provinces, there were associations of traditional rulers, such as the South-west Chiefs Conference (SWECC) from the Southwest Province and the North-west Chiefs Conference (NOWECC) from the Northwest Province. In the course of establishing these groups, the government appointed proxies and surrogates to important positions, and funnelled money to them, while the masses were strug-gling with poverty to a large extent (Bayart, 1973; Korvenonja, 1993).

This practice gave rise to "ethnic jingoism, brazen provocation and the for-mation of ethnic militias" (Fonchingong, 2004). In the Southwest Province (see Figs. 1 & 2), the focus of this chapter, the non-indigenous population, especially those from the Northwest and Western Provinces were frequently and repeatedly reminded that they were strangers, "settlers," or "come-no-goes" (translated from the Pidgin English version and referring to a difficult-to-cure disease that leads to scabbing) (Nyamnjoh & Rowlands, 1998). Near election time, the citizens would be reminded by the political elite (ministers, directors of parastatals, governors, and divisional officers) that they should go to their villages of origin to register and vote.

Amongst the multifarious elite associations, this chapter focuses on SWELA, which was formed in 1991. The Southwest Province has particular features, a brief description of which would help delineate it as a context. For example, it has a unique ecology and geology, the most obvious feature of which is Mt. Cameroon, a volcano that towers more than 4,000 meters above the coast; it is also one of the most populous provinces in Cameroon, with a large plantation complex and large-scale immigration. This high population density has not only led to pressures on arable land but has also sparked fierce resentment among groups that consider themselves indigenous toward so-called strangers (Geschiere, 2004). A large proportion of the more than 300 ethnic groups in Cameroon live in this province (Breton, 1983).

In the wake of political pluralism in 1990, the political elites of this province, in an attempt to frustrate the ambitions and will of strangers who opposed the status quo, formed an association, SWELA, in 1991, which they described as apolitical but which had political underpinnings. As a direct consequence, a new political vocabulary emerged. In local parlance (Pidgin), the immigrant labourers and their children and grandchildren were often referred to as set-tlers, strangers, and come-no-goes. The 1996 constitution did not help matters, as it made official a clause that questioned citizenship and minority rights in major city councils in Cameroon. According to this constitutional proviso, the state was empowered "to ensure the protection of minorities and reserve the rights of indigenous populations." It goes further, requiring that chairmen of the regional councils be indigenes. Although the protection of minorities (i.e., endangered minorities such as pygmies) was upheld by the United Nations, the Cameroon political elite twisted its interpretation. According to the government, minorities became indigenes/natives who were at risk *of* becoming extinct. This raised the critical question of who was a minority and who could be classified as indigenous with protected rights in a country with more than 300 ethnic groups (Breton, 1983).

## Fig. 1. Location of the South West Province in Cameroon

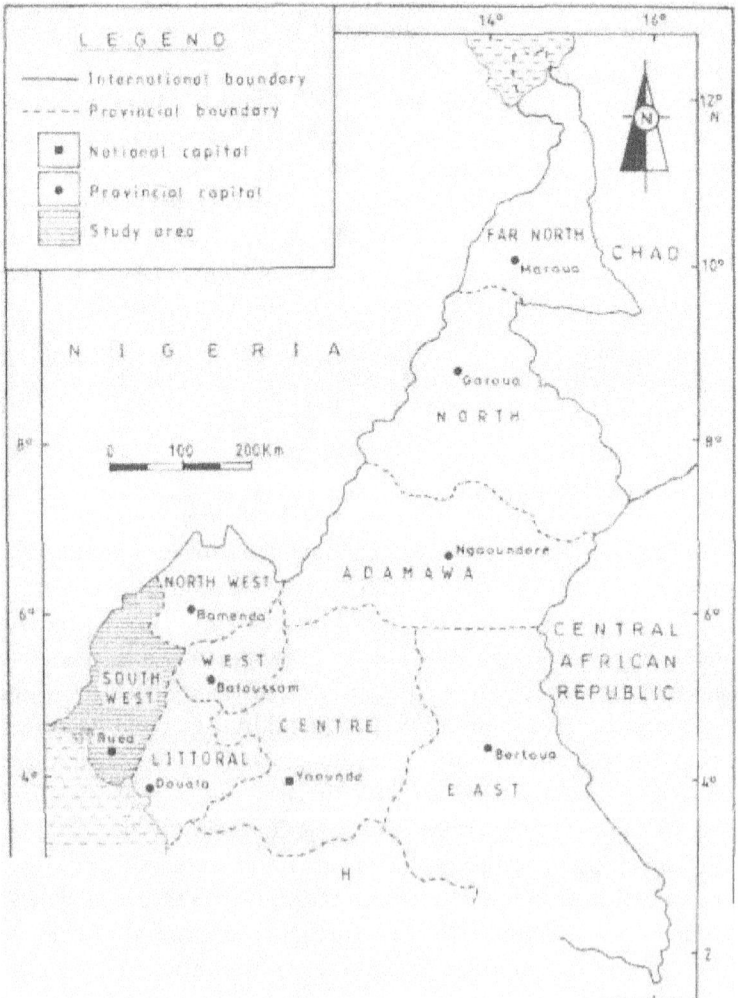

Nonetheless, Presidential Decree No. 96/031 appointed indigenes as government delegates in 10 metropolitan areas in which the Social Democratic Party (SDF), the main opposition party, won the elections. This was an attempt to put a check in place on the hegemony of non-natives in these cities.

## Fig. 2. Study area at South West Province of Cameroon.

Although this was not particular to the Southwest Province, it seems to have had the big effect in this region. For one thing, it is peculiar to the Southwest Province to hear people called either indigenous ("sons of the soil") or settlers (non-natives). In addition, the governor of the province, Peter Oben Ashu, is the only governor of 10 provincial governors in Cameroon who issued residence permits to settlers before they could vote during the legislative elections of 17 May 1997, thereby disenfranchising a good number of non-indigenes (Yenshu, 1998). This manoeuvre was intended to favour the ruling party, the Cameroon Peoples Democratic Movement (CPDM). During in this time, SWELA was born, but in the terms used by elite literature, it suffered a rumpus in 1993, at which point it segmented into its component parts. By 1997, there were three factions of SWELA, guided by inherent differences among elite groups. Nonetheless, the three factions were pro-government. An anti-government SWELA also formed, as did another group led by Akpo Mukete, the YCPDM subsec-tion president for the Meme Division and the son of chief Mukete, the traditional ruler of the Bafaw people, who believed that anybody could belong as long as he or she contributed to development. This chapter focuses on the pro-government SWELA. According to Section 3 of its constitution, SWELA's objectives include:

- Promote unity and foster development among its members and the South-west Province in general.
- Promote the socioeconomic development of the Southwest Province in line with government action.
- Provide assistance to deserving students of the Southwest Province in educational institutions.
- Promote and preserve historical and literary works of the Southwest Province.
- Organize cultural activities so as to achieve the preservation of our cul-tural heritage.
- Promote and encourage all activities likely to foster national unity.

From these, it becomes apparent that not everybody living in the Southwest Province could automatically belong to SWELA, which by extension meant that SWELA *ab initio* had started the politics of exclusivity. This opportunity was fully exploited by the government in the 1996 constitution. Moreover, its structure revealed that its activities touched the nooks and crannies of the Southwest Province, thereby actively involving the masses in its politicking. In addition, while it is difficult to identify anything political about its objectives *per se,* it is equally difficult to deny that politics played no part in its formation. For instance, SWELA was born in a political whirlwind, and was the direct result of re-splintering and reappropriating political space in English Cameroon. The region now harbouring SWELA was and is a colonial invention, branded into various sections; such as the forest zone, Cameroon Province, and the Southwest Province, by the British colonial administration and the post-independence administration. The creation and activities of SWELA do not make the elites monolithic; rather they are fighting for monopoly and hegemony over the state. In doing so, differences have occurred at various levels; though in general SWELA has become a supra-ethnic association.

Most literature on SWELA (e.g., Fonchingong, 2004; Geschiere, 2001; Konings & Nyamnjoh, 2003; Nyamnjoh & Rowlands, 1998) has treated the subject from a sociological or anthropological point of view. Those who have written from a political science and/or historical point of view (Awasom, 2003; Fonchingong, 2004) have not, in my opinion, placed enough emphasis on how the government has been using SWELA and its antecedents. The primary goal of this chapter was to fill a gap in the historiography of SWELA by limiting discussion to its historical antecedents while demonstrat-ing how this fits into ethno-regional politics and the invention of ethnicity in Cameroon. Furthermore, this chapter attempts to reconstruct the nature and dynamics of Cameroonian politics, especially in terms of elite intrigues and manipulations, and critically appraise how the Biya government has been manipulating SWELA and how SWELA (and its members) has been using the government for its own gains.

## Elites: Some Theoretical Issues and Debates

This section examines some of the views posited by scholars on the concept of elites and, an objective that is of critical importance, this study tests these views against the elite peculiarities vis-à-vis SWELA. A clear-cut definition of "elite" is very difficult to achieve and is, at times, controversial, despite its common usage in everyday parlance. The idea of elites in Africa has attracted much attention in academia, and there is an abundant literature on the topic (e.g., Barongo, 1983; Buijtenhuijs, 1978; Korvenoja, 1993; Mboukou, 1981; Mphahlele, 1959; Osaghae, 1991; van den Lindfors, 1974; Wallerstein, 1965; Wamba-dia-Wamba, 1992). Although these scholars have not agreed on a single definition, elites are generally considered those individuals who have a profound influence on society and have therefore become prime players in societal systems. Thus, this definition will be adopted for the analysis in this chapter. Important categories of elites include political, social, economic, traditional, and military, but this paper is limited to the political and traditional elites.

The analysis presented here is based largely on a theory of Fernand Braudel. Braudel (1969) proposed a two-layer model of historical time, comprising short-run time (temps court) and the *longue duree*. Instead of *longue duree*, however, this paper adopts an historical antecedent to confirm that, before the formation of SWELA, there had been another association, VIKUMA, which became the primary force behind SWEEA. The analysis herein is also informed by Bottomore's theory (Bottomore, 1976) of democracy and a plurality of elites.

Above all, this paper will employ what I call the centre-periphery theory of elites, based on the idea that differences between Yaounde elites (centre) and provincial elites (periphery) led to the break-up of SWEEA.

### Ethno-regional Rivalry and Swela's Antecedent (Vikuma)

VIKUMA stands for Victoria, Kumba, and Mamfe, the three divisions of the Cameroons under the British colonial administration (Kale, 1967). The origin of this "pressure group can be traced back to 1959 when, in the heat of political campaigning, the Kamerun National Congress (K.NC), a party with its bastion in the forest zone, was toppled by the Kamerun National Democratic Party (KNDP), based in the Bamenda grass-land zone. This was the handiwork of political and traditional elites in these divisions (Newspaper: *The Oracle*, 5(2) 2000:10-11; Konings, 2009:46-48). Aluko (2003) maintains that ethnic diversity has always been manipulated for various reasons and purposes, ranging from individual or selfish ends, to class (and other subgroup), communal sectional, and parochial interests. VIKUMA was manipulated by elites for their own selfish gain.

The rise of Foncha as the leader of the KNDP and premier of British Southern Cameroons in 1959 brought political victimization, tribalism, and nepotism at the expense of the people from the forest zone and others not affiliated with the party (Newspaper: *Cameroon Champion*, 4:12). In other words, the creed of this party was regionalism. The victimization and/or regionalism of the Foncha government was intended to address the demands of the people of the forest zone (Bakweri, Balong, Bakossi, and Bayangs, among others) in the post-plebiscite discussions (March-April, 1961) under the banner of tribal associations such as *The Molongo, Mokanya* and *Nwangoe,* who sought "a kind of separate status under the supervision of a special U. N. commission for a period of three years" (Johnson, 1970). This ran parallel to KNDP, which advocated reunification with the French Cameroons. The proponents of this idea were politically elite individuals such as E. M. L. Endeley, P. N. Motomby-Woleta, S. E. Ajebe-Sone, and N. N. Mbile. They were nationalists during the decolonization period; additionally, it should be noted that one of the problems of nationalists in West Africa, in general, was that "appeals to traditional sentiments lead to micro-nationalism of units" (Hussain, 1973).

In a situation of political victimization and growing "graffiphobia" (the word "Graffi" is used to describe individuals from the Bamenda grasslands of Cameroon), Mesumbe Walter Wilson, publisher of the *Cameroon Spokesman,* launched VIKUMA on 4 September, 1964(Newspaper: *Weekly Post,* 14-21 Feb.1994).The creation of VIKUMA was a milestone that initiated a process of ethnic formation that distinguished most South westerners (forest zone) from North westerners (grassland zone). Henceforth, South westerners were increasingly perceived as a people with natural ter-ritorial and cultural boundaries. However, it also gave South westerners a sense of common destiny, and launched a common front against "institutionalized" discrimination.

As early as 11 October, 1963, before VIKUMA was even established, a meeting was held in Dr. Endeley's house; in attendance were Mbile, Henry Namata Elangwe, D. B. Monyongo, and Ajebe-

Sone, the political elite of the coastal zone. They resolved to "fight so hard that the vice president [of the Federal Republic] and the Prime Minister [of West Cameroon] should not all be from the Bamenda grassfields",(Ngoh,1999).

VIKUMA was radical, and provided a forum for discussing problems of the coastal people or forest zone. At the top of its agenda was the idea of freedom from the "Bamenda oligarchy." According to its founder, Walter Wilson, the Bamenda people were not sincere about reunification, and had accepted it only on condition that they would dominate it (Newspaper: *Weekly Post,* 1994; *Cameroons Spokesman,* 1964).Wilson reported that between 1949 and 1954 Southern Cameroons had two separate provinces: the Cameroons Province, corresponding to the present-day Southwest Province, and the Bamenda Province, presently the Northwest Province. When Southern Cameroons was granted the status of an autonomous region in 1954, the Bamenda people protested that they did not want the Bamenda Province to be abolished (Kale, 1967). They argued that, with Dr. Endeley as leader of governmental affairs, political power was in the hands of those from the Cameroons Province, which in turn would make defending their own interests difficult. As a compromise, the British opened a liaison office in Bamenda to aid the Bamenda Province. Once Foncha broke away from the KNC and formed the KNDP in 1955, the liaison office automatically disappeared, because the Bamenda political elites did not feel threatened by Buea. VIKUMA was formed, therefore, to fight for the same issues that the Bamenda people had been fighting for between 1954 and 1959, when they were not in power. VIKUMA, however, went further in that they advocated a territorial reorganization of the Cameroon Federation on ethnic lines, regrouping the present South-west with the Littoral Provinces, and headquartering it in Kumba, as well as the present Northwest and the West Provinces, headquartering it in Bafoussam (Newspaper: *Cameroon Mirror,* 1965).

Other than emphasising the chauvinistic and jingoist attitudes of the VIKUMA president, the foregoing sets out constructions of ethnicity by the various ethnic elites. To say that the Bamenda people protested the autonomous region of 1954 is largely an error with respect to Cameroon historiography (Fanso, 1988; Johnson, 1970;

Kale, 1967; Mbile, 2000; Ngoh, 2001). It also shows that the conglomeration of the Grand SAWA movement, ethnically-related coastal elite of the Southwest and neighbouring Francophone Littoral Province, on the basis of common feelings of exploitation and domination by grassland settlers in the 1990s, is something that had long been whispered among VIKUMA members (Konings & Nyamnjoh, 2003; Yenshu, 2006). Above all, it portrays in no small way the creation of ethnicity by the colonial administration and the continuation of an appropriation of political space by the post-colonial elites. However, VIKUMA was dissolved in 1965 when its founder joined the Cameroon United Congress (CUC) as publicity secretary. This was striking, because the party was led by Solomon Tandeng Muna, who was from the grassland region (Northwest). Perhaps the demise of VIKUMA fell in line with historical trends that included an ambivalent perception of modernization as, on the one hand, essentially destructive and alien and, on the other hand, a provider of scarce beneficial resources (Yenshu, 1998). The coastal people were the first to come in contact with the Europeans, and their attitudes towards modernization have fluctuated, from collaboration when there were benefits to be reaped to protest and opposition when it became invasive. Thus, VIKUMA and SWELA were formed to protest the Bamenda hegemony, thereby inventing an ethnic association. Whatever the case, VIKUMA's politics created, first and foremost, a keen sense of self-awareness within the present-day Southwest Province. Second, it helped launch several subsequent elite associations, including SWELA. Third, VIKUMA and SWELA were created to compete for scarce resources, whether economic, social, or political, with kin from the Northwest.

The 1970-1980 decade was one of despair and disillusionment for the South-west elites, who claimed they had been marginalized. This feeling stemmed from the fact that all prime ministers of West Cameroon succeeding E. M. L. Endeley had been from the Bamenda grasslands (LeVine, 1965). In response, the Southwest elites either blackmailed other South westerners to gain favours from their francophone-dominated political masters, or remained silent while their resources were "raped". It should be noted upfront that the Southwest Province has many natural resources, including, rubber, cocoa, banana, timber and even crude oil deposits. It also played host to the only oil refinery in the country. As a result the region's political/traditional elites fell and still feel that they should play an important role in the national politics. Consequently, a frustration bordering on alienation began to form, as claimed by these political elites. To prevent this trend developing further, a pressure group that would fight for the interests of the Southwest became necessary. SWELA was born, therefore, in 1991 as a continuation of VIKUMA, and as a re-appropriation of political space.

## Developments Leading to the Formation of Swela

SWELA was born out of the desire by Southwest elites for collective leadership that would articulate ethnic and provincial interests, both of which they felt had become increasingly marginalized in political, economic, and social domains. Most South westerners had come to realize that by pursuing Anglophone/Francophone logic, the distribution of value within the system would not favour them, for the North westerners were the dominant Anglophone group, and they usually received most of the benefits reserved for the Anglophone community (Newspaper: *Weekly Post,* 14-21 February 1994). In other words, SWELA was established to compete for social, political, and economic resources against the Northwest elite, who were in an advantageous position as the majority group. The fact that they were not well represented in the government, but provided much of the country's resources (e.g., oil, rubber, bananas, palms, and tea) is similar to the situation of the Niger Delta minorities of Nigeria (Isumonah, 2001). But unlike the South westerners the indigenous population of the Niger Delta has resorted to force in order to gain a fair share of their resources.

The idea of an elite association was given an additional fillip with the elec-tion of President Biya in 1982; this was part of the effort to create a propaganda weapon on the part of the regime so that it could demonstrate popular consensus and consolidate its power. In this light, a group of Southwest elites, mostly high-level players in the Cameroon National Union party in Buea (headquarters of the Southwest Province) and Yaounde (capital of" Cameroon) signed motions of support for Biya during his conflict in 1983 with Ahidjo, his predecessor (Fanso, 1988). It should be noted that the Cameroon

National Union Party (CNU) was formed in 1966 after all opposition parties had been dissolved. The name of that party was quickly changed in 1984 to the Cameroon Peoples Democratic Movement.

However, the Biya-Ahidjo fracas was apparently sparked when Ahidjo attempted to unseat Biya in a coup d'état, which was ultimately prevented (Takougang & Krieger, 1998). After the fracas, Biya decided to test his popularity by calling a snap presidential election in 1983. During the election, many ethnic elite associations sent motions of support to Biya. (Oben & Akoko, 2004).

The first major challenge that emphasised the necessity for a powerful SWELA was the Pamol Plantation Du Cameroun (PAMOL) crisis. Pamol was an agricultural plantation established in 1952 by the Unilever Brothers in Ndian Division, South west Province.(see Konings, 1988a) In October 1987, it was rumoured that PAMOL was to go on voluntary liquidation (Nyamnjoh, 1997), and that a group of Northwest business magnates, namely Daniel A. Nangah, Martin Che, and Wilie Nango Kimbeng (one time Deputy Manager), had tendered to buy it. In response, a meeting of more than 60 South west elite individuals in Yaounde gathered at the residence of Minister Martin Kima (Newspaper: *Cameroon Tribune*, December 1983). A Southwest-based company, CAMAGRI, was asked to tender and compete on-the-spot, and registered with shares of 50.000 francs (US$100 each). Two major players involved in this effort were Minister Ogork Ntui, board member of PAMOL, and Governor Enow Tanjong. The purchase of PAMOL, which South westerners viewed as tantamount to mortgaging most of the fertile lands of Ndian and even rendering some 6,000 South westerners unemployed, rekindled the concerns of Southwest elites(Newspaper: *Weekly Post*, 28 February-7 March 1994).

But what helped galvanize the coming together of the Southwest political icons were two outstanding events that occurred in 1988. First, the death of veteran politician E. M. L. Endeley took place; this was followed by the resignation of Solomon Tandeng Muna, speaker of the National Assembly (Ngoh, 1987). The death of Endeley was a great loss for the Southwest elites, who were aware of the great vacuum he had left behind, and of the fact that there was no-one in the province who could fill that gap. Consequently, there was a need for a pressure group to provide collective leadership in the absence of any respectable Southwest spokesman.

The resignation of Muna was even more serious than the death of Endeley, because the South westerners had been planning on the basis of him being the speaker of the National Assembly. They had even held, rightly or wrongly, that W. N. O. Effiom or Thomas Ebongalame, old and experienced politicians of the province could fill the gap (Newspaper: *Weekly Post*, 1994). However, the Northwest elite smartly positioned Achidi Achu and Joseph Awunti, from Mezam, and former vice minister of agriculture and minister, in charge of parliamentary relations. Whether by design, accident, or political expediency, Biya then appointed Fonka Shang Lawrence, from the Northwest Province. This appointment either demonstrated how impotent the Southwest lobbying group was, or Biya's lack of faith in them. It further pointed to the fact that the Southwest elite individuals residing in the capital of Yaounde showed little tact when it came to defending the position of the Southwest Province. The appointment also aggravated the conflicted relations of South westerners over state resources in relation to Northwesterners. The appointment of Fonka, in any case, showed the Southwest elites that it was necessary to base an elite association in the province, not in Yaounde. It will appear that the Southwest elites had sound case to make in relation to this political marginalization, primarily because they had never designated a prime minister or a speaker of the national assembly since Endeley faded from the political stage in 1958. Foncha for example, was succeeded by Solomon Tandeng Muna, Lawrence Fonka Shang and then Simon Achidi Achu, all of whom came from the Bamenda grassland area.

In 1989, with increased political tension following the end of the Cold War, a wind of change blew across Cameroon, leading to widespread student riots in the over-populated University of Yaounde (Nyamnjoh, 1997). This political convulsion led to the creation of the only Anglo-Saxon University of Buea following Decree No.92/034, of 19 January 1993, which organised the University of Buea on Anglo-Saxon Lines. The University of Buea, far from "papering the cracks" opened up new fissures. The differences between the "Northwest and Southwest became clearer and deeper as well.

The creation of the University of Buea helped give birth to SWELA. In fact, immediately following its establishment, a group of Southwest elites residing in Yaounde, led by Yaounde University

Vice Chancellor Dr. Peter Agbor Tabi, sent a motion of thanks to the government of Paul Biya. Suspicious that the North-west elites might attempt to decentralize the new university for their own benefit, Tabi's group, called SWEG, held a series of meetings and sent a memorandum to the Minister of Higher Education condemning any moves for decentralization. The birth of SWELA had thus begun.

**The Birth of Swela**
SWELA was fostered into existence primarily by five prominent South-westerners, namely, David M. Iyok, Barrister Abraham T. Enaw, and chiefs Emmanuel Tabe Egbe, Ephraim Enoni, and Fomenky. Their power lay in the fact that most had already been working with the government in at least a ministerial role. The exception was David M. Iyok, who was a financial baron and founding manager of a paper company (SAMCO). Moreover, some had gone by traditional titles, such as chief, which, by implication, meant that they were custodians of culture and of the people. It was at Chief Egbe's house that these prominent Southwest elite individuals, and others such as Iyok, organized as a single entity to address the issue of the University of Buea. Then, on 25 May 1991, the Southwest Elite Forum summoned another meeting in Victoria Hall that laid the foundation of SWELA. Jointly organized by Chief Inoni and Limbe Urban Council Mayor Dan Matute, it brought together 38 people, drawn from Yaounde, Limbe, Buea, Douala, and Kumba (Newspaper: *Cameroon Post*, 1-8 December 1993).

Although this meeting had no defined agenda, Chief Inoni emphasized the necessity to unite and speak with one voice to solidify the strategic position of the Southwest Province and fight for its interests. In this way, he helped bridge Yaounde to the provincial forces of SWELA. One week later, another meeting took place (31 May 1991), attended by 99 retired "sons of the soil," including Mola Njoh Litumbe and former ambassador Fossung. The aim of the meeting was to identify the major problems of the province, and its importance lay in the fact that it dispatched a six-man delegation to the All Anglophone Conference held in Buea, 3-6 June 1991.

D. M. lyok also played a very important role in the establishment of SWELA. He helped give the forum a provincial dimension, and acted more or less as the propaganda hub through which all patrons and elders were contacted. Moreover, he sensitized many others, including barristers Nkongho and Chief Tabetando in Douala, and Chief Fomenky, Chief Raymond Beseka, Ekinde Sona, Dr. Nzume, and Dr. Meboka in Kumba to the importance of a provincial association (Newspaper: *Weekly Post,* 1994). Furthermore, he largely organized the next crucial meeting, which took place on 8 June in Kumba. The Kumba meeting brought together some 300 people, and essentially served as the inaugural meeting of SWELA. Lawyer A. T. Enaw chaired the meeting, and S. N. Dioh was Vice Chairman. Lawyer Edjua proposed the name of Southwest Elites Association, and a constitutional draft committee was created, consisting of lawyer Eseme, justice Bawak, and S. N. Dioh.

Another meeting in Limbe (6 July, 1991), which attracted a crowd of 1,500 people, closely followed the Kumba meeting. The issues of membership of the 11th province in SWELA, and a 10-state federation for Cameroon were discussed. The issue of the 11th province is really link to an enigma and has been gaining currency in Cameroon body politics since the 1990s. The 11th province is largely composed of inhabitants who, as a result of colonialism, cannot be identified as purely Anglophone nor Francophones. (For more on the enigmatic 11th Province in Cameroon see Geschiere, 2001:93-108; Yanou, 2007:25-27; Percival, 2008:2; Newspaper: *Postwatch*, 30 December 1999).

The constitution of SWELA was adopted, and on 7 August 1991, SWELA was officially registered in conformity with law No. 90-153 with the Senior Divi-sional Officer of Kumba. Kumba thus became the birthplace of SWELA. On 21 August 1991, the association was recognized and legitimized by the indigenes of the Southwest province. Thus SWELA was established in a context of ethnic, civil, economic, political, and social marginalization for the Southwest Province. Its future was uncertain.

### Internal Wrangling Within Swela

In contrast to the euphoria and conviviality at the inception of SWELA, it was greeted with suspicion and obstruction both within and outside the prov-ince. The first major problem that confronted

SWELA was that of the relationship between the Yaounde Southwest Elites and those based in the province. As previously mentioned, Dr. Endeley had succeeded in providing leadership from the province (not Yaounde). The creation of SWELA signified a rejection of the Yaounde elites, who were accused of not addressing the interests of the South-west people. Henceforth, Southwest interests were to be articulated from the province, and not Yaounde.

This rift between the provincial and Yaounde elites manifested in late September, 1991, during President Biya's visit to the Southwest Province. The presidential protocol reserved some 100 invitations for SWELA. Unfortunately, all were withheld by a Southwest minister who never delivered them to the national executive (Newspaper: *The Oracle*, 1(1) 1991: 15-18). Consequently, the protem chairperson and vice chair and secretaries could not sit in the grand stand where the president sat (Newspaper: *Weekly Post*, 1998 No. 0052:10)

The second conflict arose when a SWELA delegation comprising Abraham T. Enaw, lawyer Edjua, Nnoko Mbele, and Dr. George Atem were prevented by Southwest minister Benjamin Itoe from having an audience with the president on 28 September 1991. In a personal communication with George Atem on 10 October 2003 in his house he told me that the biggest shock in that respect was that it had been their contemporaries from Yaounde who had prevented them from seeing the President. "I knew things were rapidly changing in SWELA never to be the same again", he said while twisting his forehead. Following these events, and Minister Ogork Ntui's anti-national conference campaign it became clear that the Yaounde elite would attempt to hijack the association for their own ends (For more on National Conference in Africa see, Robinson, 1994:575:610; Joseph, 1998: 3-17; Ihohnvbere, 1996: 15-35). The words of SWELA Secretary General A. T. Enaw, spoken at the Mamfe conference (December 1991), clearly sums up the situation:

> The visit of the Head of State to the Southwest Province on 27 and 28 September 1991 has now become history but there are lessons to be learnt by all members of SWELA. The first problem of determination is where is the seat of SWELA located? Is it located in Yaounde the national capital of the

Republic of Cameroon or is it located in the South West Province.... Let no man or group of people give the impression that SWELA is under their armpit and they control it through a remote control (Newspaper: *The Oracle,* 1(1) 1991:15-18).

The tussle in SWELA had started, arising primarily out of competition with the state over resources. The conflict was mainly political because, to a large extent, Yaounde was the seat of government and the Yaounde elite felt that they should control SWELA. It should be noted that factional struggle within a pressure group and or party, such as that which took place in the Kenyan African National Union between 1969 and 1996 (Buijtenhuijs, 1978), is common. This competition illustrates what I call centre-periphery theory, or vertical competition among elites, which is simply the struggle between elites in the centre and those on the periphery (i.e., in the provinces).

The second major challenge, which permanently fractured SWELA, stemmed from the newly created Southwest Chiefs Conference (SWECC). Its members were custodians of the people, and most of them (e.g., Mukete, Endeley, Elangwe, Molongwe, Arrey, and Manga) had been active politicians. They considered themselves core elites; most represented conservative ideals, and all were staunch members of the ruling party, the Cameroon People's Democratic Movement (CPDM). Including them in SWELA, with special roles as national executives and advisers at chapters and branches, transformed these traditional elites into political elites, and marked the beginning of SWELA's decomposition. The differences that occurred within SWELA illustrate, in concrete terms, inter-elite competition stemming from a political elite's desire to identify with the state and control political and economic resources (Chazan *et.al.*1992). Such situations are more acute in impoverished regions, because poverty often drives the ambition and activities of elites (Barongo, 1983).

Compounding SWELA's problems was the general perception that it was a xenophobic association aimed at containing the settler population, which was mostly from the Northwest Province (Delancey, 1974). However, it also incurred the wrath of the Southwest French Cameroon settler population. The French settler population was a colonial product; they had immigrated to the British Southern Cameroon to avoid harsh colonial policies by the French and terrorist activities by the *Union des Populations du Cameroon* (UPC). They settled, married, and gave birth to children who were educated in the English ways. In 1991, most of them were painfully reminded that they had never been officially belonged to the Southwest province. (See Nyamnjoh and Geschiere, 1998). There was some basis for this, and it appeared to accord with the intentions of the government in that some of the French Cameroonians who had settled in the Southwest Province long before had been refused membership to the association (Geschiere, 2001). This conflict over the political centre was a major force leading to the split of SWELA. However, other factors were equally important.

First, Cameroon is made up of more than 250 ethnic groups, and SWELA included Orocko, Bayangi, Bakweri, Bangwa, Bassosi, Bakossi, Bafaw, Balong, and Mbo, with six administrative divisions. Although SWELA was a supra-ethnic association, it nonetheless had individual indigenes that fought for their own specific group's interests. Second, SWELA was born in a political whirl-wind by politically hungry leaders, many of whom intended to use it as a shield for their own political ends. In the heat of the multiparty political tempest, and from within SWELA, emerged opposition leaders as well as those of the ruling government. The differences became acute, contributing to its eventual fragmentation. Third, the nuances between traditionally educated elites and politicians *per se* were never differentiated from the onset. Some traditional elites claimed to be superior and saw SWELA as an arm of SWECC. Finally, the organization put into place the "derivative policy," which meant that the more a region contributes to national development in terms of natural resources, the more it is rewarded in terms of development. However, in practice, some regions contributed more resources but were not rewarded while others contributed less but were rewarded. Consequently, the elites from regions that contributed more but received less felt slighted and such sentiments fragmented SWELA.

## Swela Goes Plural

The first step towards the plurality of SWELA took place in 1992, before its 1993 split, during the general assembly meeting in Mudemba, Ndian division, shortly after the 1992 elections. During the assembly, it was stated *inter alia* that "SWELA addresses any government present and future to consider the development of the South West Province as it's preoccupation as a condition for our continual loyalty." (Newspaper: *The Oracle*, 1(2) May 1992: 33).This statement declared that if the government showed any interest in the development of the Southwest Province, then SWELA was going to show unalloyed loyalty and vice versa. This did not go unnoticed by smart politicians, who exploited the opportunity.

The opportune moment came with the death of SWELA's Secretary General, A. T. Enaw in May 1993. Konings & Nyamnjoh (2003: 112) maintained that "the military brutalities in the South West Province during the 1993 government anti-smuggling campaign led to a split in SWELA." While not overtly rejecting this notion, the death of the Secretary General may have had more to do with the split than the anti-smuggling campaign, because through that death a power vacuum was created.

Martin Nkemngu, who was vice secretary general, thought he was constitutionally granted the right to fill the space, pending future elections. However, "Nnoko Mbelle did not consider Nkemngu a true Southwesterner, even though he was Bafaw, a prominent ethnic group in the Southwest Province and was in close contact with the Yaounde elites. The general assembly in Menji, Lebialem division, on December, 1993, provided the occasion for Nnoko Mbelle to boy-cott it, alongside his supporters, calling it illegal. He went ahead to form his own faction (Newspaper: *The Herald*, 15-18 June 1995).

Nnoko Mbelle's opinion that Nkemngu was not a true South westerner stemmed from the fact that the former belonged to the Social Democratic Front (SDF), an opposition party with a strong following in the Northwest and Western Provinces (For more on SDF see, Ngoh, 2004; Fombad and Fonyam, 2004; Kreiger, 2006; Takougang and Krieger, 2000). Secondly, Nkemngu comes from the Lebialem division, which is halfway into the grasslands and the forest zone. Thus, Mbelle felt that Nkemngu had never been generally elected. It was in this environment that SWELA suffered a split, with Mbelle heading a faction. Although he was taken to court several times, all such efforts were as effective as a "storm in a tea cup" (Newspapers: Weekly Post, 16-23 October 1995:6; Weekly Post, 4-10 November 1994:6; The Herald, 6-8 February 1995:6; The Oracle, 2 (1), January 1997:12)

Nnoko Mbelle's faction of SWELA had highly-placed CPDM agents, and was thus called a pro-government SWELA, or SWELA 11, given that there is no clear-cut distinction between the party and the state in Cameroon. These high-level CPDM members included Emmanuel Tabi Egbe (Roving Ambassador), Peter Agbor Tabi (Minister of Higher Education), John Ebong Ngolle (Minister), Ephraim Inoni (Minister), and Caven Nnoko Mbelle (Secretary General). There were also prominent Southwest chiefs, such as Mola Samuel Endeley and Nfon Victor Mukete (Konings & Nyamnjoh, 2003; also see Newspaper: *The Herald*, 21-24 July 1994). The handwriting was clearly on the wall; SWELA had gone plural, and the government had penetrated its fabric.

The governor of the Southwest Province, Peter Oben Ashu, was one of the first to identify with the pro-government SWELA, because of his CPDM's leanings. He began by giving his blessings to the executive, and promised to grant their request to hold their general assembly in Kumba, but remarked that "these days nothing goes for nothing."(Newspaper: *The Herald:* 23-25 May 1994:6) He apparently wanted his guests to provide him with assurances that they would reverse the disastrous fortunes of the ruling CPDM in the coming elections by capturing councils for the CPDM in the Southwest Province. He regretted the fact that the CPDM had a very poor standing in the province.

Reacting to Governor Peter Oben Ashu's attendance at the "illegal" SWELA meeting in Kumba, Peter Agbor Tabi remarked that:

> It is unfortunate that we are in a country where on the one hand the governor expects state institutions to be respected, and on the other hand, he deliberately supports a recalcitrant individual in breaking the law. This is an unfortunate situation, which we see as double standards, and I do not think any right thinking Cameroonian will condone with such behaviour (Newspaper: *The Herald*, 31 March-3 April 1994:3).

It is difficult to accept Tabi's position, given that he too was in the government and at the same time a member of SWELA. Perhaps he was just playing the role of biblical "Pontius Pilatus" who despite the fact that he washed his hands to show his innocence in the crucifixion of Christ will still hand over the crown of thorns to his enemies.

The SWELA II faction executive, however, accepted the governor's condition, promising to contribute 16 million francs (US$ 35,000) to sponsor the CPDM campaign in the Province at the upcoming elections. As a mark of further assurance of the SWELA II acceptance to support the CPDM election campaign, the creation of action committees was discussed, with one of them called the "committee of strategy." What had become clear was that SWELA had missed its original objective and *ipso facto* had been hijacked by the government. Yet the members of SWELA were also expecting to gain from the government. They started seeing benefits following the 1996 municipal elections, in which Nnoko Mbelle was appointed the government delegate for Kumba urban council. His rival, Martin Nkemngu, was placed on a 'punitive' transfer to Yaounde as an ordinary member of staff of CAMNEWS. This was essentially a punishment, because he had formerly been the head of CAMNEWS in Buea (Geschiere, 2001). However, this point is still debatable, because the act of transferring civil servants in Cameroon is a government action.

The Yaounde-based pro-government SWELA faction also suffered a rumpus, over the admission of Southwest candidates into Ecole Normale Superieure (ENS) (Newspaper: *The Herald*, 1995). Each of the six divisions of the Southwest Province were entitled to 10 places in the ENS, with the Manyu division having 26 extra seats, because the Minister of Higher Education, Peter Agbor Tabi, came from that division. The list was arranged and handed over to Chief Ephraim Inoni, Assistant Secretary General at the presidency; John Ebong Ngolle, Minister for Special Duties at the Presidency; and Peter Agbor Tabi, who was to be the final arbiter of the list. Much to the chagrin of these elites, out of 83 candidates from the Southwest, only 10 came from their list. This was particu-larly unusual, because the ENS had been established to train professional teach-ers, who were admitted on merit alone.

But because the Minister of Higher Education belonged to the Yaounde SWELA, the political elites of the province wanted to make a fortune out of this prestigious institution by grabbing more state resources for it.

In response, the executives resigned *en masse*, leading to another split. This intra-elite competition stemmed from conflict over who would gain access to a greater share of state resources. Peter Agbor Tabi, who had been promoted from Vice Chancellor of Yaounde University to the Minister of Higher Education, was held responsible for letting down the Southwest Province with respect to the utilization of state resources. Whatever the case, the pro-government SWELA never failed to support the government during election campaigns.

**The Fortunes of Swela**
The political campaigns of the pro-government SWELA were at times direct and at times indirect. Regardless of their technique, what became clear was that most citizens did not exercise their civic responsibility. When Governor Peter Oben Ashu gave his blessings to the 'rebel' faction of SWELA, it was on con-dition that they would help redress the poor CPDM situation in the Southwest Province. The SWELA II group responded positively, promising to contribute 16 million francs to sponsor the CPDM campaigns in the province at the upcom-ing council elections. This constituted a tacit entente between pro-government SWELA and the government, and it demonstrated that the latter was dedicated to campaigning.

After being appointed Prime Minister of Cameroon in 1996, Peter Mafany Musonge's words at his reception left nothing in doubt. Amongst other things, he said, "Biya has scratched our back and we shall certainly scratch the Head of State's back thoroughly when the time comes" (Konings & Nyamnjoh, 2003). Musonge was emphasizing that Biya should be rewarded abundantly during the next elections for appointing him Prime Minister, an appointment the Southwest had not experienced since 1958. Assistant Secretary General of the pro-government SWELA, Norbert Nangiy Mbile, also used the appointment of Musonge to campaign: "Therefore he [Musonge] has to be assured of the support of all South Westerners.

The support has to be oral, total and convincingly expressed in the forthcoming elections. Only then can we expect him to deliver the goods"(Newspaper: *The Herald*, 1995; Star *Headlines*, 20 November 1996:1-7; *The Herald*, 11-12 November 1996:3).

On 12 March 1997, SWECC Secretary General Atem Ebako called upon South westerners to support the ruling party in the forthcoming parliamentary elections (Newspaper: *Cameroon Post*, 12-18 November 1996:1-3). He said:

> Our communities especially those in Fako and Meme divisions, are swarmed by Cameroonians from other places and provinces.... It is not possible to have Cameroonians who are not indigenous in the Southwest Province to become representatives of South Westerners at local councils, parliament and government. This aspect of the evolution of the political life of the Southwest Province which became very obvious after the 21 January 1996 municipal elections is most repulsive, resentful indignant and preoccupying. Our choice is clear as we stated in the general Assembly Meeting in Kumba on 8 March 1997, We call on all South Westerners of voting age to register and vote massively for the candidates of the CPDM party of president Paul Biya at the forthcoming parliamentary elections (Newspaper: *The Oracle*, 2(1), January 1997:23).

However, the pro-government SWELA also used intimidation to campaign. Governor Peter Oben Ashu did not mince words when he said that the South-west was ready to go to war to keep Biya, Musonge, and the CPDM partly in power. He went ahead and issued a war cry on the eve of the 1997 parliamentary elections, declaring, "we are ready to fight to the last man to maintain our son as prime minister. This is the time for all South Westerners to be ready to die or survive. We have the South Westerners and what we need now is only satisfaction and social amenities. The Southwest is satisfied with what it has and anyone who is not here to safe guard the interests of the province should immediately pack to his home" (Newspaper: *Pilot Magazine*, May 1997).

As a direct consequence of this campaign, the CPDM scored a spectacular victory in the Southwest Province, via manipulating elites: to reward the pro-government SWELA, many individuals from the Southwest were either appointed into new positions or confirmed in their old positions. It was on this direct connection with the comfortable position of the CPDM in the South-west Province that "SWELA had to re-focus its objectives.

## Conclusion

The multiparty politics in Cameroon in the early 1990s helped create and shape elite associations along ethnic lines. Some were born with the government's blessing, while the government hijacked others. Nonetheless, these elite associations reflected the ethnic and geographical boundaries of Cameroon. SWELA *per se* was established in the Southwest Province with an initially, superficially, apolitical objective. The real objective, however, was to contain the political and economic *modus operandi,* of the grasslanders in this province. After its birth in 1991, the government hijacked it for its own ends. This study has demonstrated that while SWELA had been using the government for its own ends, the government had also used SWELA to retain power. It has also been argued that SWELA was created by a small number of elites to foster and defend their whims and caprices within the authoritarian regime of Paul Biya. This chapter has also proposed that SWELA and its historical antecedents may be linked to concepts of ethno regional politics and the construction of ethnicity. The democratic process remains an illusion in Cameroon, and in most of black Africa, mainly because of the self-interested nature of elite groups, but also because of government manipulation of the masses via elite proxies and surrogates. The next chapter examines the telephone operators in British Southern Cameroons.

# Chapter Six

## "The Voice of the Voiceless": Telephone and Telephone Operators in Anglophone Cameroon

### Introduction

This chapter aims to write the social history which focuses on the telephone and telephone operators in erstwhile British Southern Cameroons from the pre-colonial to the end of the Mandate period. The last decades of the $20^{th}$ Century witnessed an explosion of mobile/cell phones communication in Cameroon, and the world at large. In certain quarters this has been dubbed as a revolution. Although some studies have been earned out with regards to this phenomenon in Jamaica, Asia and Nigeria, documented literature is amazingly absent in Anglophone Cameroon. This essay goes beyond "the-now" phenomenon of cell phone communication to capture the overall nascent history of telephone and those who greased the telephone machinery in former British Southern Cameroons during the British Mandate period from 1922 to 1939 with hindsight. A dearth of primary material was consulted in the National Archives Buea, Cameroon and Public Records Office archives in Kew, London and from these repositories; the paper contends that the initial telephone systems were elitist in nature and that the operators who were indigenous Africans played an important role in keeping the administrative machinery of colonialism moving. In areas where the telephone lines stopped, human beings acted as telephone lines by carrying important mails and load on their heads.

**TWO things** have inspired me to write this chapter: The first one is the eclipse of the cell phone in the Bamenda metropolis, Cameroon, between 16 and 17 of April 2007 hindering subscribers from calling their love ones, making business contacts and gambling difficult. The cell phone and the internet had been introduced to Bamenda just less than a decade although generally in the Bamenda Grasslands and Southwest Cameroon which make up the Anglophone Cameroon, it has been well entrenched within decade and a half.

The second thing is that from the 29 to the 30[1] of August 2007 I attended a workshop in Bamenda organized by the African Studies Centre Leiden on the impact of Information Communication Technology (ICTs)' From the discussions it was clearer that the population had become so obsessed with the internet and cell phones to such an extent that it could be said that it has become part of people's anatomy. People have internalized it and they used it for different purposes-to date their fiancés to coordinate stealing, to communicate with principals of schools who are managing the schools where their children are schooling; to make emergency calls; make death announcements, transact businesses, scamming etc. As a matter of fact, the use of the cell phone in Anglophone Cameroon is quite multifarious and fascinating and gives the impression that before the cell phone there was no other way of communication.

Like in Jamaica and Nigeria (Horst and Miller, 2006 and Smith 2006:497-523), cell phones are dramatically changing the lives and livelihoods of people in this part of the world- erstwhile Anglophone Cameroon. According to Nyamnjoh (2005),

> In the Bamenda Grassfields, for example, marriages, feasts; funerals, *crydie,* and village development initiatives can no longer pass by any Grassfielder simply because they are in the Diaspora. The cell phone has become like the long arm of the village leadership, capable of reaching even the most distant sons and daughters of the soil trapped in urban spaces

It is a truism that the cell phone has changed the social landscape of the town and even its people and environs. Yellow is the colour of communication as the advertisements of MTN, Airtime etc show it is ubiquitous. The visibility of the cell phone technology and the urgency to use it everywhere in the streets of Bamenda, Buea, Kumba, Limbe and all main towns in this region etc make one conclude that owning a cell phone in Cameroon in general and Anglophone Cameroon in particular and using it, is a given. The presence of a cell phone is also internalized in people's behaviours, in the material expressions of their communication culture. There is no street without people carrying cell phones. The presence of the cell phone is not concealable. In church, meeting houses, taxis, beer parlours, coffee farms, the markets, toilets etc phones are being used with ring tones usually high. The 48 hour obfuscation left the Bamenda town in a bewailing state. Nothing appeared moving as people appeared marking time and crumbling and looking gloomy. The question that quickly came to mind as what use to happen when there was no cell phone? How did people communicate in the past?

Drawing largely from primary sources in the National Archives Buea (NAB) Southwest Cameroon, and Public Records Office archives, Kew, London, and some secondary sources this chapter attempts to show in a way how the telephone evolved from the pre-colonial to colonial period. I find this more imperative because as Ali Mazrui (1969:661-676), puts it, "we study history in order to discover how we have come to be where we are" It is because of this that it is important for us to know how messages were sent and received before the mobile phone came and who were the people responsible in facilitating the messages?

For purposes of clarity I have decided to situate the chapter within pre-colonial and colonial boundaries. The pre-colonial period refers to that indigenous period before Cameroon officially became a German colony in July 1884. It is interesting to study this period because it is important to know how technologically advanced people were in Africa in general and Cameroon in particular before colonialism with special focus on the telephone. The period will also act as antecedent, to the period in focus. This will also go a long way to debunk the imperialistic jargons that all in Africa was savage chaos before imperialism. The colonial period will roughly run from c.1884 when the Germans colonised Cameroon to 1916 when they were muscled out. The Mandate period will roughly run from 1922 - 1939 under the British colonial administration. The importance of the Mandate period lies in the fact that we need to know how the communication voice has evolved and how elitist it was as compared to the present cell phone world that respects no class and status. It is also intriguing to me to document those who generally became known as telephone operators/clerks. These people have been ignored in the historical discourses of British Southern Cameroons. Who were these indigenes who facilitated the operational machines and kept the colonial machinery moving with focus to the telephone and how did the colonial masters view the telephone operators?

The role played by colonial clerks, translators and interpreters has not been given enough attention in Cameroon historiography by either Cameroonian scholars or other scholars. But elsewhere in Africa attention has been given. In 2006 a brilliant number of essays were jointly published in an edited volume by Benjamin N. Lawrence, Emily Lynn Osborn and Richard L. Roberts. These essays included articles on issues as diverse as interpreters, interpolators, intermediaries, court clerks in most of Africa South of the Sahara. The fundamental issues that cut across in the volume were the fact that Africans were collaborators in the expansion and consolidation of European colonial empire and they were in fact also instrumental in the day to day running of the colonial empire (Lawrence, 2006:4-6). Unfortunately, this book has no contribution on telephone and telephone operators neither in colonial West Cameroon nor in the rest of Africa. This chapter therefore will attempt to fill a lacuna in the general historiography of the telephone and telephone operators during the pre-colonial, colonial and Mandate periods. My departure point will be, to first situate a brief history of the Anglophone Cameroon. I will then proceed to examine the telephone during the pre-colonial period. The second section will examine the telephone during the German period. Part three will be the Mandate period. Part four will consist of the telephone operators. The essay ends with a conclusion.

## Brief History of Anglophone Cameroon

The area known today as Anglophone Cameroon was known before 1961 as the British Southern Cameroons. After the First World War the German Kamerun was partitioned between France and Britain. France took 4/5 of the territory while Britain took 1/5. Britain later administered her own portion as one of the provinces of the Eastern Region of Nigeria. For administrative and pecuniary convenience, Britain partitioned her sphere of German Cameroon into two parts: a northern section which in Cameroon and international jargon became besprinkled the Northern Cameroons and a southern section which became known as the British Southern Cameroons.

British Southern Cameroons consists of that portion of the former German Cameroons which, under Article 22, Part 1 of the Treaty of Versailles with Germany, the principal allied and

Associated Powers agreed should be administered under a mandate by his Britannic Majesty (CO 583/159/220, Report on British Cameroons for 1927, 1928, No.220, Public records Office, PRO, Kew, London). It was situated on the coast between the Cross River on the West and the Mungo River on the East. The sphere of former German Cameroon under the French administration was on the East and Nigeria was on the West. In 1938, this territory had a total surface area of 16,581 square miles and a population of 445,735 people (File Ba (1938)2 Cameroons Province: Notes on the League of Nations Report, 1938, National Archives Buea) British Southern Cameroons, which is the focus of this chapter, is inhabited by Bantu-speaking peoples. Along the coast in Victoria division are the Bakweri, some of whom claim a common ancestor with the Duala. Besides, there are also the Mboko, the Isuwu and the Wovea who although claiming different origins, have several cultural similarities with the Bakweri. Further inland, in Kumba Division are the Balong, Bafaw, Bakundu, Bakossi, Oroko and the Mbo (Report on Victoria Division, Cameroons Province, written for the League of Nations by A.R. Whitman, District Officer, September 20th, 1921, National Archives Buea).

In the Mamfe Division, the indigenous peoples are the Korup, the Ejagham, the Boki, the Banyang, the Bauchi, Awachi and Nchumbere (Report on Victoria Division, Cameroons Province, written for the League of Nations by A.R. Whitman, District Officer, September 20th, 1921, National Archives Buea).

The Victoria, Kumba and Mamfe divisions were usually referred to as the forest region of the Southern Cameroons because most of the natural ecology is the forest.

Further inland stretching almost 450 kilometres is found open grassland which the German earlier explorers called the Bamenda Grassfields although it is interspersed with forest shrubs in the valleys. The peoples of this region are grouped into chiefdoms or Fondom and some claim dynastic connections with the Tikars of the northern part of Cameroon a point which is much contested by recent researchers. Generally, this sub region is made up of four ethnic groups. The Tikars include: Bafut, Nso, Kom, Bum, Fungom, Oku and Babanki (See E.G. Hawkesworth, 1923, Assessment Report on Banso District, Bamenda Division; R.J. Hook, 1924, An

Intelligence Report on the Associated Village Groups occupying the Bafut Native Authority Area of the Bamenda Division of Cameroons Province; G.V. Evans, An Assessment Report on the Bikom. National Archives, Buea). There are also the Widikum who do not possess strong chiefdoms. They include: Essimbi, Beba Befang, Mankon, Ngemba, Ngie and Mogamo (See F.A. Goodliffe, 1949, The Bali Re-organisation Report, National Archives Buea; R.J.Hook, 1934, An Intelligence Report on the Ngie Clan of the Widikum Tribe inhabiting the Bamenda Division of the Cameroon Province; Arnette, 1925, Assessment Report on the Mogamow and Ngemba Areas of Bamenda Division, National Archives, Buea). There are the Chambas who include: Bali-Nyonga, Bali-Kumbat, Bali Gangsin, Bali-Gashu and Bali-Gham (CO 323, General 1922 vol.5, 890 Foreign Office, Jan-July League of Nations Mandate, Public Records Office, Kew, London).

The British implemented the system of Indirect Rule in Southern Cameroons which was also the system they had implemented in Nigeria. This was because they had decided to administer this portion as an integral part of Nigeria. The administrators who facilitated the British colonial administration were often known as District Officers and Assistant District Officers. The system of Indirect Rule was proclaimed in Cameroon in 1921 and it only became operational in 1922 (C.J.A. Gregg, An Assessment Report on the Meta Clan of Bamenda Division, Cameroons Province, 1924, National Archives, Buea). It is within this geographical space that the chapter attempts to examine the social history of telephone within the pre-colonial, colonial and Mandate periods.

**The Pre-colonial Period**
This period usually refers to the time before European colonisation. It is also viewed as the period when African civilization was *in situ*. During this period, the talking drum was so important to African polities as a means of sending out messages. Anglophone Cameroon was not an exception. The messages could be coded and decoded depending on the person who was sending the message and who was receiving the message. This was the most popular way of dispatching information. Writing in 1924 C. J. A. Gregg, Assistant Divisional Officer for Bamenda Division captured this point. He said *inter alia:*

The Meta drums used for tapping out messages and dancing are hollowed out of a tree trunk; they may be any size. The length is three times the diameter, and the native commences by cutting sound holes very like those in the belly of a fiddle. Through these sound holes, he uses a crude native chisel to hollow the drum. The Melas are expert in tapping out messages and it is wonderful how many names, alarms and matters of everyday life, arranged in ancient times are remembered. The writer lost a dog, and the native drummer was able to find its whereabouts by means of his drumming. It was never necessary to call a village head by messengers, the drum was sufficient. Anyone able to receive the messages of the Meta drums would be "an fait" with the greater part of the remembered clan history. At first the assessing officer was mystified: the drumming seemed a language in itself, and it was not until the natives were tested practically that things became clear. The chief was asked to call a certain man, but it was found to be impossible because his name was not arranged for the drum. A new village drum can always be called by drum, or a son of a man of standing, in the following manner: The village is called up, then the name of the father or a well remembered ancestor, and so on to the newly arranged name, which soon becomes familiar, through constant repletion, through out the clan. The drumming is a sort of Morse code without the alphabet. Each message has to be separately arranged, and the by frequent use it is remembered .In effect, it is the same as when a telegraph operator becomes expert he ceases to think of dots and dashes or when recognizing the national anthem we never think of the notes of music which go to make up the tune. There is a system of dots and dashes tapped out on the different notes given each side of the drum sound holes, and when the native speaks the message he says: A.Ger.Ger.Ger.Ger. Ger. A. in a very similar way to us imitating the sound of the dots and dashes we hear on the buzzer. The members of *kwifon* are called by beating a tattoo on the iron gongs and when they have assembled legislation begins after the debate a member dons masked dress and announces the order to the town, the chief by this time is back in his compound and with resignation says "kwifon has spoken" thus clearing himself of the responsibility of an unpopular order.. ..

The above quotation from Gregg shows how important the drum was in a pre-colonial setting in sending out messages. It also reveals the technology informed in the making of the drum and more importantly he compares the drum specialist with a telephone operator. This shows the extent to which some pre-colonial polities were advanced in their original setting. It also shows how creative Africans were before the colonial era. The story of the talking drum was also reported by another Assistant District Officer in Kom (File Ad2 (1927) Bikom Assessment Report, National Archives Buea). Rudin (1938:112) attested that,

> ...evidence of high intelligence in the native is the use of the drum woven together in Southern Cameroons for sending messages. The two tones of the drum woven together by intricate rhythm made it possible to send by night as well as 'by day any message that could be spoken. It was an achievement in communication far superior to that of the Whiteman before the invention of the telegraph.

However, the talking drum suffered a shortcoming. Its messages could not go very far and so it was geographically limited in comparison with the modern telephone.

Apart from the talking drums some polities in the Grasslands of Cameroon used the *mobu* or *wa-mabu* to send royal messages. This type of masquerades was renowned for speed and could cover a considerable distance within a very short time. They were exceptionally used in the palace and therefore were not accessed by the general public. The Fon, who was the spiritual and executive head of a Kingdom, could use the royal spear to send a message to his colleague and only the colleague will understand the meaning bestowed in the royal spear (File Ad(1934), W.M. Bridges, Reassessment Report on Banso District, Bamenda Division, National Archives, Buea) During inter-tribal wars, which became quite common in the 19th Century the big war drum and the chief war horn were used to summoned village warriors in most parts of Anglophone Cameroon (Nyamnjoh, 1998).

In certain areas traditional dressing was designed in a way that it communicated a language. Grass was often tied in particular forms by people and send to their kith and kin. Only those who received the grass could decode the message which was found in the grass (File Rg (1917)12 Bamenda Division: Flag Post Service-Recommendations for continuance of, 1917; Memorandum, No.3709/1918, from the Resident, Cameroon Province to Engineer –in-chief, Post and Telegraph Buea, 8th January 1918, National Archives, Buea).This system although with its shortcomings, proved to be very effective within the indigenous system. The system was supplanted by the European colonialists, especially the Germans and later the British. The two colonial masters used the local chiefs to supply them with labour to prop up what I have preferred to call "human telephone lines". The next section of the chapter will therefore turn to this human telephone lines which was instituted by the Germans.

**The Flag Post System, 1884-1917: Human Telephone Lines?**
The Germans officially annexed Cameroon in July 1884 and looked for various ways and means to effectively implement their administration. Around the coast, which was the loci of plantation agriculture and other administrative services, they used the trunk line telephones. Further in land, they decided to use human beings in a way that could only be comparable to the telephone trunklines. One of these ways was the flag-post system which was used in the transportation of mails by relay running. This became known as the flag post system. This was systems which relay runners carried letters from village to village by day and night. Huts were constructed at convenient intervals and the chiefs of the village had to supply boys free of charge to carry the mails (Memorandum, No.901/10 from Resident's Office, Buea, 23 December 1916-Kumba-Victoria-Ossidinge- Chang and Bamenda, National Archives, Bamenda).

Each flag post was provided with a flag for the hut itself and it was to save confusion if each District or Division had different coloured flags or marks on the envelopes and attached to the postal packet. For instance, Bamenda-Red; Chang-White; Ossidinge-Blue; Kumba-Blue and White; Buea Red and White (File Ag (1917), memorandum from Resident's Office, E.C. Duff, Resident,

127

Cameroon Province, Buea, National Archives, Buea). The colours were more compelling because most of those who worked in the flag post huts could not read and write and so they could only recognise colours on the postal packages. Notwithstanding, the flag post system turned out to be very advantageous.

In 1916, the Resident of the Cameroon Province, E.G. Duff, summarized the advantage of the flag post system in the following words: "The flag post system is infinitely quicker as economical-a day's run by ordinary messenger can rarely be over 15 miles, owing to the hills, rivers and forests compared with 60 miles by flag post relays...(Memorandum No.339/15/17 from Assistant District Officers' Office, Kumba on Tour at Buea, the 28th June 1917 to the Resident Buea, titled "Flag Posts, National Archives, Buea). Further in 1917, it was reported that the flag post system had speed and also helped the Administrative Control. The presence of the post was a constant reminder to the villagers of Government's activities and enabled local troubles to be reported at once (Confidential Report, No.1/1916, Bamenda, 28th February 1916 by G.S. Podevin, Resident Cameroons Province; File Ba (1922)2 Report for the League of the Nations, 1922; File Fg (1923), Report on the Bamenda Division of the Cameroons Province for the League of Nations, by Mr. W.E. Hunt, District Officer, National Archives, Buea).

These two advantages explain the advantages of the flag post system but not its necessity. The *raison d'être* of that system was pegged on the fact that telephone lines were inadequate to reach all the administrative nooks and crannies of the territory and where they reached they were more often than not always problematic. Again as already said, the flag post system was to act as a constant reminder of the people of the presence of colonial administration of which the chief was the liaison officer. Any squabbles were immediately reported to the central administration by the mail runners.

The distances often covered by those working at the flag post were deliciously unbelievable. For instance the Bamenda-Tinto-Ossidinge axis was 95 miles and took 3 to 4 days; Bamenda to Buea 205 miles took 16 days via Tinto 63 miles and Kumba 153 miles; Bamenda to Nso 95 miles and to Nkambe 3 to 4 days; Bamenda to Kentu 120 miles and took 7 days and Bamenda to

Chang 55 miles and took 4 days (File Ag (1917)2, Flag Post System National Archives Buea). In these flag post huts, messages were communicated faster and at whatever hour of the day or night a letter or message was received it was the duty of that post to forward it onto the next without any delay whatever (Ibid.)

Embarrassingly, "there was no hardship attached to the work. For this reason the workers are not paid and there are no charges for the maintenance of the buildings." (For the history of plantation labour in this region see Konings, 1993 and CO 936/18 International Trusteeship Affairs in British Cameroons IRD, Public Records Office, Kew, London). It is unthinkable that such distances could be covered for no remuneration and the colonial administration contend itself that there was no need to pay the people. What comes out clearer is the fact that the flag post system was instituted for economic reasons, perhaps it was to cut down the cost of running the colony. It also goes only to support the view that there was hard labour or ill treatment of the colonized during this period and in many forms.

Whatever the case if the communication voice was meant to transmit information from one end to another using the telephone lines, the bulk of work carried out by the workers of the flag post system did just that. Therefore it is plausible to say that the human beings were used as telephone lines more so because they had to transmit the information from one end to another at whatever period or hour of the day. When the Germans were muscled out, the British took over the territory and "effectively" used the telephone trunklines.

## The Telephone in the Mandate Period, 1917-1939
The earliest time to get documented sources about the telephone in Anglophone Cameroon under the British was in September 1917.This is through a letter from the manager, Mokundange Plantation Cameroon Province to the supervisor of plantation, Bota. "I beg to complain of the annoyance caused by the misuse of the telephone. I am constantly being cabled away from my work and chap to answer the phone to find a private conversation going on between natives. The chief offenders are the telephone man, Robert at Bota and a man called Stephen at Isongo" (File Ag (1920) Misuse

of Telephone: Complaint regarding 8th October 1917; File No. 132/1920 Telephone Service Complaints Re, September 11, 1920, National Archives Buea). The telephone was an elitist thing reserved only for the Europeans and mostly used for business transaction.

Once an indigene was caught using the telephone he/she was punished. On 8th October 1917, Overseer Stephen was fined 2 pounds which was to be deducted from his salary because he had been caught using the phone on the 2nd of October 1917 (File No.1492/1925, Report for the League of Nations, 1925, National Archives, Buea). Yet the indigenes were quite important for the overall running of the telephone communication which was used by the European administration.

Apart from using the phone for business transactions, the colonial administration profusely used the telephone for other administrative purposes. According to the League of Nations Report for 1925, the Divisional Officers for the Mamfe, Kumba, Bamenda communicated with the Resident in Lagos using the telephone and emphasizing the importance of the telephone to the well being of the colonial administration in many ways. (File Ba (1922)2 Report for the League of Nations 1922; Report on the Bamenda Division of Cameroons Province for the League of Nations by W.E. Hunt, National Archives Buea).

In 1920, there was a direct telephone communication line with Buea and Lagos through Chang, formerly under the British but transferred to the French Cameroons in July 1920. The line was throughout put up by Nigerian Telegraph Department but within the Cameroons Province although it was of a temporary nature and more liable to interruptions (Report on the Victoria Division, Cameroons Province written for the League by A.R. Whitman, District Officer, 30th September, 1921; Report for the League of Nations on Ossidinge Division, 17 May 1921 by Rutherfoord, District Officer, National Archives, Buea). Buea appeared to be the hub of the telephone system thence lines radiated to Victoria, through Kumba to Tinto and thence to Ossidinge on the one hand and to Bamenda on the other. The Cameroon system was connected with the main Nigerian system via Ossidinge and Odubra, on the Cross River in the Calabar Province (File Ba (1923)2 Report for the League of Nations, 1923, National Archives, Buea). In 1923 there were thirteen indigenous telegraph workers (File Ba (1931)6, Notes on Cameroons for the League of Nations Report, 1931, National Archives, Buea).

Wireless installations were effected in May, 1931 and as a result there was great improvement in telephony communication with Nigeria. The head of the installations was in Buea and by the end of the year preparations were in place for the early installations of similar plant of smaller power in Mamfe and Bamenda. These smaller installations were to be in touch with Buea. The Buea installation was sufficiently powerful to keep regular communication with Lagos (Report by His Majesty Government in the United Kingdom of Great Britain and Northern Ireland to the Council of the League of Nations on the Administration of the Cameroons Under British Mandates for the year, 1927, National Archives, Buea).

In 1936, some seventeen lines were installed during the year. Five trunk lines were connected to the telephone exchange areas of Victoria, Tiko, Buea and they worked satisfactorily. The first wireless stations at Buea, Mamfe, and Bamenda also gave good services (Letter No.M.P.No.E. 204/1921, National Archives, Buea). Despite the "good services" it was not long that the telephone lines were soon broken down.

The frequencies of letters to the effect that phones had broken down were many and varied and mostly came from the top management of the plantations that had been opened in the coastal area of Cameroon by the Germans, amongst others. On 11th August 1921, the supervisor of plantations, Ekona wrote directly to the Inspector of Posts and Telegraphs. Amongst other things he said: "The telephone between Ekona and Tiko has been out of order for the past three days and I shall be obliged if you will give the matter attention (File No.58/16 Telephone Service Et/1921, 11 August 1921, National Archives, Buea) Again on September 27, 1921, he wrote [hat "The Bota-Bibundi telephone line is still out of order and I shall be obliged if you will give the matter your early attention (Letter No.73/5/1927 from the Resident Cameroons Province, Edward Arnett to the Secretary of Southern Provinces on 11th January 1927, National Archives, Buea). According to the Resident, Cameroon province, "During the past twelve months I have repeatedly represented the urgent need of an ordinarily efficient telegraph line in the British Territory because of the frequent breakdown of the present one...." (Extract of a letter No. D.93/21 Dated 11th October 1921 from the Manager, Debunscha Estate to the Supervisor of plantations, National Archives, Buea).

On 11 October 1921 the bad situation of the telephone system was captured more forcefully. In a letter from the Manager, Debunscha Estate, G. Waldau, to the Supervisor of plantations he said:

> One of the reasons why the Telephone do not function by so far well now as before is of course that a part of the material is old and warned out. Another reason very likely lies in the system which I think one can call the old system more complete than the present. Now all stations between Bibundi and Bota are connected by one single wire. Anyone speaking on that line is heard by all the others and the telephone boys never can resist the temptation to listen which weakens the current. It is nearly daily experience that at one moment the person speaking is heard clearly, in the next as speaking in a very far distance. As one does not know who is listening, the thing cannot be stopped. Before the war there was exchange station in Isongo from where a double-wire went to Debundscha and the other to Oechelhausen. Everybody speaking had to go through the exchange and there was no listening and no interruption by others as now often is the case. The Telephone was then so good. Bibundi could speak with Buea even Douala. Such long distance conversations were ordered in Victoria and arranged before hand and a certain hour fixed (CO 583/164/6, Telephone Service 1929, Public Records Office, Kew, London).

The constant breakdown suffered by telephone trunk line installations led to an emergency visit of the Post Master General, H.M. Woolley to the Cameroons in 1925. At the end of the visit, he pointed out that the telephone system was extremely unsatisfactory and entirely of a makeshift character (Letter No.199/21, Tiko Plantation to the supervisor of Plantations, Ekona, September 1920, National Archives Buea). If one was to compare the telephone system with the flag post system by any parameter it will be noted that the latter was quite effective. That notwithstanding, the constant breakdowns of the telephones showed in a way that the colonial administration was not used to this technology. If they were embarrassed then the need and ultimate employment of Africans of little western technical education was more a dilemma to the colonial administration. This was because they could not ignore them in the administration. The next section will handle the telephone operators.

## Telephone Operators: A Colonial Dilemma?

From the beginning the Colonial administration justified her policies on grounds of civilizing the heathen and constantly referred to Africans as hewers of wood and drawers of water. The colonial venture was to spread glad tidings to those who had no "access through the gates of civilization". It was not long that the Africans who had been ridiculed became a *sine qua nan* to the success of the colonial enterprise. One of these areas was in the telephone clerks or operators.

No sooner had they been employed than they were seen by the same administration as misusing the telephones, absent from work and constantly referred to as black useless niggers. This partly stemmed from the fact that the operators were unfamiliar with the newly installed dialling systems of the telephone industry and partly because the telephone clerks or office attendants took the phones as "toys". In 1920, Mr. Findlay, one of the managers in the plantations wrote about the telephone operators in the following words:

> I regret that I have again to complain of inattention and incivility on the part of the Telephone exchange clerks at Buea. My clerk at Molyko has under my instructions, been trying all day to get through to Bota to ask for an engine to be sent to carry cacao from Molyko to Bota and has failed, the answer from Buea always being that Victoria was engage. I tried myself about noon and get the same answer "Victoria engaged". Presuming under the circumstances that this was untrue, I asked who was then on the Victoria line and was told in an insolent manner that I could not know....The Molyko clerk has as yet, 5-p.m. failed to get through further than Buea, and now Buea refuses to answer repeated calls either from Molyko or Ekona. That the line through to Bota is in order is evident from the fact that Mr. Cameron was speaking from

Bota to Ekona this afternoon. The result of our failure to get into communication with Bota will be the loss of probably 50 pounds or ever through the wet cacao having to remain in the trucks at Molyko for an unduly period. That such a serious loss should result from the inattention of insolent black clerks is beyond words of condemnation, and I trust that the seriousness of their offence will be suitably impressed upon them (From Correspondence Manager, Bota/ Victoria to Supervisor of Plantations Ekona Letter No. 1218/16 of 1st August 1923, National Archives, Buea).

(Sigd)A.J.Findlay<br>Manager

The quotation demonstrates yet another form of hierarchy that existed within the colonial telephony world-that of master and telephone clerk, or office boy. The employment of the services of telephone operators was somehow the last resort to the British colonial administration because their services were needed and it is ironical that the same administrators turned around and portrayed the operators in a derogatory manner. The telephone operators were not only subjected to but abusive language, they were also constantly accused of neglect of duty. On 1st August 1923 the manager of Bota plantations wrote to Supervisor of plantations Ekona thus:

This morning at regular intervals of 10 minutes, I tried from 7 am to 8:30am to get through to you by telephone. Each time Buea exchange informed me there was no reply from Molyko. I had the same difficulty on Monday last when I tried to transmit a cablegram from Beynis over the phone. I am reporting this to you because either Buea Exchange does not try to put me through or else Molyko Office will not reply. In view of the conflicting reasons given for non-connection (at one time I am told 'no reply' and-a few minutes later 'line engaged'. It is evident there is lack of attention somewhere. At 1 pm I got Molyko who replied 'can't get Ekona'(Ibid.)

In another instance on 13 December 1922, the manager of Tiko wrote to the supervisor of plantations in the following words:

Will you please use your authority and lay before the Director of Posts and Telegraphs the very culpable neglect of duty of the Exchange Telephone clerks at Victoria. At times the line may be out of order and then of course it is not possible to communicate with Victoria but at other times the exchange clerk obstinately refuses to respond to ones call, although perhaps only 5 minutes before my clerk may have got him. I can hear the clerks often talking and joking amidst roars of laughter when all the time (File Rg (1923)5 Telephone Service (Victoria Division) 16 January 1923; Letter from Manager Tiko Frank Pyatt to supervisor of plantations, Bota, 13 December 1922, National Archives, Buea).

In another instance on 13 December 1922, the manager of Tiko wrote to the supervisor of plantations in the following words:

Will you please use your authority and lay before the Director of Posts and Telegraphs the very capable neglect of duty of the Exchange Telephone clerks at Victoria. At times the line may be out of order and then of course it is not possible to communicate with Victoria but at other times the exchange clerk obstinately refuses to respond to ones call, although perhaps only 5 minutes before my clerk may have got him. I can hear the clerks often talking and joking amidst roars of laughter when all that am trying to get is the exchange. They seem to do just as they like and there is a great lack of supervision. The Marine Engineer here complaints of the same treatment (File Rg (1923), 3 Post Offices: Victoria and Buea re-Telephone and Co. Victoria Division, 1923, National Archives, Buea).

The complaints against the telephone operators continued flowing. In December 1923 the manager of Bimbia wrote to the supervisor of plantations in a letter captioned Telephones. In that letter he said amongst other things:

This afternoon I wanted to speak with the marine on the telephone and as it takes such a long time to be connected I told my boy to get through for me. After ringing he got the Victoria exchange at once but when he asked for the marine the operator called him "a bloody fool" several times. He tried

> again after about three minute's interval and still could not get through. When I have finished with the marine I got through to Victoria to ask for an explanation. The operator was impertinent and when I said "I shall report this" he answered "oh well, you can do as you like about that" and cut me off (Ibid.)

The above quotation cannot be taken uncritically. First, it shows how laborious it took to make a call. Second, and paradoxically, the introduction of colonial education to update the indigenes with functional knowledge also turned out in the way they were answering their masters. Thirdly, it re-emphasizes the master-servant rapport and hierarchy that went with the telephone during this period, it is also interesting to note that the operators after acquiring the education felt that their status had changed; they thought that they were like their masters. This comes out quite eloquently in the reply of the operator who does so with a bit of arrogance, "oh well, you can do as you like about that".

## Conclusion

The last decades of the 20th Century witnessed an explosion of the cell phones. People have internalized the usage and in most cases it has become part of people's anatomy. This essay has not preoccupied itself with the cell phones per se. It has rather taken a step backward to trace the evolution of the telephone from the pre-colonial through the colonial to the mandate period in erstwhile British Cameroons. The essay has also examined the flag post system which was put in place by the Germans and the use of telephone operators or clerks during the mandate period. In the operation of the former, the paper has contended that there was the master-servant relationship and in the latter the colonial administrators took the workers for granted. In both cases the colonial administration showed in all probability that they were out to exploit the labour found in the colony to the advantage of the metropole. The paper has filled a hiatus in the historiography of Cameroon by examining the telephone from pre-colonial to the Mandate period. Finally, the chapter in a way has closed the gap that existed in the telephony world before the advent of the cell phone. The next chapter is focused on civil society in Cameroon.

# Chapter Seven

## The Dilemma of Civil Society in Cameroon since 1990: Which Way Forward?

### Introduction

The role of civil society in societal transformation and nation - Building in Cameroon has been compromised by political and social strictures created during three decades of autocratic rule that still underline the practical and moral workings of the state today. Civil society remains mired in societal cleavages that find expression in parochial tendencies ranging from ethnicism to regionalism. As a result civil society's ability to mobilise all and sundry towards a meaningful democratic culture is limited. In this context the quest for good governance has remained, for the vast majority of Cameroonians, a platitudinous Utopia. This chapter argues that only a civil society that transcends narrow social and political boundaries and identifies with the daily and legitimate struggles of ordinary citizens can serve as a signpost pointing towards meaningful quantitative and qualitative development in Cameroon.

Like most countries in Africa, Cameroon is a colonial construct. It has its specificities and paradoxes, which can be quite mesmerizing. I believe that Cameroon is one place where logic does not always have its way, where outcomes are never predictable. For example, in one country where the price of bread is raised by 33 cents, the whole country is expected to go up in flames. But in Cameroon, the currency is devalued by 100 percent, followed immediately by a 70 percent slash in civil service salaries, and not a finger is raised. Cameroon tops the Transparency International world corruption index one year (1998) and is sufficiently comfortable with that performance to repeat the feat the next year. To the best of this writer's knowledge Cameroon is also the only country in the world with two constitutions, each operating according to the whims and caprices of the ruling government. The country is a vastly wealthy triangle, yet its entry into the Heavily Indebted Poor Coun-tries Initiative (HIPC) is celebrated as a national achievement. Cameroon is one of only a few countries in Africa to have had three colonial masters, Germany, France and Britain, and has serpentine through Anglo-French trusteeship, federalism and the unitary state, to what is today just the state.

Even natural cataclysms respect the strange ways of this country. Mount Cameroon, West Africa's highest peak, erupted in 1999, but the lava flew down the slopes away from human settlements. The one-kilometre-wide blazing liquid flew downhill for close to fifteen kilometres, destroying all the vegetation, but stopped a few metres from a hotel complex and within sight of the country's only oil refinery. At the end, not a single person died. Cameroon has the poorest football pitches anywhere in Africa but the richest football fame in Africa, having won the African Cup of Nations in 1984, 1988, 2000 and 2002. It has participated in the World Cup finals five times and is the first African country to reach the quarterfinals of the World Cup. Geographically, even Cameroon's location is ambiguous, with an English-speaking sector located in West Africa and a French-speaking sector in Central Africa

Since 1961 Cameroon has been ruled by two presidents who combined the tactics of divide and rule, Machiavellianism and outright totalitarianism, except for the brief period of 1982 to 1984 when Paul Biya, the second president, introduced a dicey policy of liberalism, but when a coup d'état threatened to eliminate him he became a dictator, and any signs of opposition were driven underground.

However dictatorial rule did not go on forever. The last decade of the twentieth century witnessed debates over the role of citizens in societal transformation in Cameroon in particular and Africa in general after the end of the Cold War, the reunification of Germany and the failure of African totalitarian states to provide minimum social, economic and political resources to their citizens. More especially, the question was pivoted around what strategies, options and forces could be amalgamated to promote democratic transition within internationally recognised norms while taking into consideration the local history and the political and economic peculiarities of the state (Mbuagbo and Fru 2003).

In Cameroon the challenge of civil society has been to create awareness in citizens that will encourage them to take responsibility for their individual and collective destinies (Mbuagbo and Robert

2004). Unfortunately the liberties of citizens as found in the constitution have remained so far a dead letter. Civil society is fractured, and the flavour of its vibrancy has gone sour. In any ordinary sense civil society deals with day-to-day operations of livelihood and one should be able to talk of civil society when it has an impact on the society; if not it should be left out. However civil society has occasioned endless disputes over definitions and its study in Africa has made great strides (Comaroff and Comaroff 1999; Kasfir 1998; Sitoe 1998; Osaghae 1994). Some scholars have seen civil society in terms of advancing democracy and disciplining the state to ensure that citizen interest is taken seriously and greater civil and political participation is fostered (Carothers 2000). Others have conceived of civil society as a critical element of democratisation, arguing that the current failure of the process of democratisation in Africa hinges in part on the failure of states to respond to the pressing demands of their people (Fatten Jr. 1995). Yet others see civil society as more or less imaginary: 'outside of the sociological, historical and cultural events of its imagination, the existence or non-existence of civil society is not significant' (Tester 1992). Still others see civil soci-ety as the process by which society seeks to breach and counteract the simultaneous 'totalisation' unleashed by the state (Bayart 1989). Finally others simply define civil society as 'new spaces for communication and discussion over which the state have no control' (Monga 1998). The various definitions are limited by the fact that they are mostly Eurocentric, and this Eurocentrism has been difficult to deconstruct (Bratton 1989; Harbeson *et. al.* 1994).

However the definitions are useful to the present work in that they provide some paradigms which will be borrowed and tasted. In the light of these definition civil society can be broadly understood as the do-main of non-kinship-based contractual relations comprising interest groups such as traditional rulers, credit and development associations, student unions, Bar Associations, journalists' associations, religious groups and women and men in the informal sector. These organisations should exist independent of the state but at the same time be prime movers of societal dynamism. Civil society generally is pegged on a number of themes: to foster the spirit of democracy (Ceesay 1998), to mediate relations between the state and society, to set the rules and ethos of public conduct and to ensure that the state reflects the social reality and is committed to the pursuance of the public good (Osaghae 1998).

The role of civil society in societal transformation and nation-building in Cameroon has been compromised by political and social strictures deriving from three decades of autocratic rule that still underpin the practical and moral workings of the state. Civil society remains mired in societal cleavages that find expression in parochial tendencies ranging from neo-patrimonialism, clientelism, ethnicism to regional-ism, thereby limiting its ability to mobilise citizens towards a meaningful democratic culture. In these circumstances the quest for good governance remains, for the vast majority, a platitudinous Utopia. The pith and kernel of this chapter is to examine the roots of civil society in Cameroon and its impact on the Cameroon body politic and to chart a new way forward for civil society in Cameroon.

## Ingredients of Cameroon's Civil Society

Awasom (2005) has delineated the various components of Cameroon's civil society in the 1990s to avoid 'ambiguities'. My analysis does not in a strict sense, diverge from this approach but will re-interpret it with available data where needed. Civil society is made up of individuals who have an interest in redressing political, economic and social abnormalities in the society. Students press their demands through student bodies, workers through trade unions or professional groupings, market traders through the formal or informal market associations and so forth. Sometimes several groups combine to make demands on government, especially when the levels of immiseration and deprivation have become unbearable (Osaghae 1994).

Civil society in Cameroon became quite vocal in the 1990s and was bent on 'opening and expanding the political space' (Awasom 2005). Various groups and organisations thirsted for freedom, justice, and good governance. The initial group was made up of students and workers' unions. They emerged as the main critics of the regime against a back-drop of degrading conditions in the lone state university, the University of Yaounde, opened in 1961 more for political than academic objectives. By 1990 the university hosted more than 32,000 students, well beyond its carrying capacity, while graduates remained unemployed and the economy was souring (Nyamnjoh 1997; Konings and Nyamnjoh 1997). Traditional societies then emerged in the names of *Takembeng* and *Anlu* and were quite instrumental during the civil disobedience campaign and the post-October 1992 election results. As a matter of fact, democracy in Cameroon since 1990 has gone only as far as the political ritual of holding elections, all of which have been marred by gross irregularities and blatant disregard of the fundamental principles of democratic electioneering (Nyamnjoh 1999; Mbuagbo and Robert 2004)

Religious groups and organizations also became vibrant and vocal elements of civil society. The Bishops of the Bamenda ecclesiastical province addressed a 25-point letter to the Prime Minister, Simon Achidi Achu, asking the government to address the political, social and economic situation of the state. The church, especially the Roman Catholic Church, even went as far as hosting political party activities considered anathema by the state. A case in point was the All Anglophone Conference, which took place in Mount Mary Health Centre, Buea, in April 1993. The Social Democratic Front convention was also held several times at the church centre, Big Mankon, a citadel of the Ecclesiastical province. Even the Episcopal Conference came out with statements that were critical of the government.

Meanwhile the Cameroon Bar Association did not remain numb in the search for a democratic space. When its ex-president and a prominent Barrister, John Mandengue Yondo Black, was arrested for attempting to form a party as a counterpoise to the ruling party, the arrest aroused the rage of the public against the state and brought demands for a more plural society to their apogee (Awasorn 2005). Eventually political parties were given an official stamp by a regime that had held tight to change. These political parties questioned and criticized the lack of political space. On January 9, 1991, the *Cameroon Tribune* news-paper published a list of 41 registered political parties which by 2004 went far above 180 (Awasom 2005).

These were some of the constituents of civil society in Cameroon by the 1990s. So vibrant was it that the archaic and totalitarian system prevailing since 1961 was condemned to kowtow. However, judging from its *modus operandi* today, it is doubtful whether the civil society represents any way forward towards meaningful development in Cameroon. Does it really exist at all in Cameroon as the extant literature conceives it (Mbuagbo and Robert 2004; Orkin 1995; Abdelrahman 2000)? Before attempting an answer, it is imperative for us to examine the roots of civil society in Cameroon. The next section therefore will examine the dynamics that gave rise to civil society.

## The Roots of Civil Society in Cameroon in the 1990s

The roots of civil society in Cameroon in the 1990s are many and can be appreciated under economic, social and political rubrics. Economically the situation in Cameroon was bad and was aptly captured by a headline in *La Nouvelle Expression,* February 24-27, 1995, 'La Banque mondiale prevoit: encore un demi siecle de misere pour les Camerounaise' ('The World Bank Forecasts: Another Half-Century of Misery for Cameroonians').

Takougang and Krieger (1998) also provide very illuminating figures from the General Agreement on Tariffs (GATT) text on Cameroon. According to them real gross domestic product (GDP) per capita rose from US$500 in 1970 to a peak near US$1,200 in 1986 but then fell back to US$500 by 1994. The ratio of external debt to GDP doubled from 1986 to 1992. Net foreign direct investment from all sources of US$300 million in 1985 became an US$80 million disinvestment in 1990, while there was a 40 percent drop in the value of petroleum exports between 1990 and 1993. Between 1988 and 1992, Cameroon's productivity was the worst among forty-one African countries from which statistics were available (Takougang and Krieger 1998). The public service sector was in fragments. Salaries, which in any case were not paid regularly, dropped from 70 to 60 percent between 1990 and 1995. Retirement was enforced at 55 years of age or before, with pensions as problematic as salaries. The 100 percent CFA Franc devaluation in 1994 took an additional toll.

Socially, unemployment was near astronomical figures. University and professional—school graduates hardly picked up any job. Besides, an end to student bursaries and the introduction of school or registration fees caused untold disillusionment and frustration to many who could not even afford their 'daily bread'. To add insults to injuries, many Cameroonians were deported from Gabon and felt more or less frustrated in Cameroon, as they remained idle, causing untold misery to themselves and their families.

Politically, the Cameroon of the 1990s was pegged on divide and rule, neo-patrimonialism, the politics of the belly, prebendalism, patronage, clientelism and so on (Bayart 1993; Konings and Nyamnjoh 1997; Nyamnjoh 1999). The net effect was that the Cameroon society, from the height of the state's level, appeared to be peopled exclusively by a multitude of private individuals chosen for their loyalty to the state rather than on merit. The Beti ethnic group from which the President comes occupied almost all the important positions in government (Poggi 1978; Ndembiyembe 1997). These people embezzled state resources without a 'modicum of morality' (Wiredu 1998).

The situation becomes very positive for the emergence of the civil society when absolute monarchical rule is arbitrary. Also, authoritarian regimes, in de-politicising as well as atomising their respective societies, give rise to civil societies. Here the civil society designs itself to change government policies (Holm et al. 1996; O'Donnel and Schmitter 1991). The Cameroon situation in the 1990s illustrates all the seeds that are necessary for a civil society to germinate. The next section of this chapter will look at the ramifications of civil society on the body politic of Cameroon.

## The Ramifications of Civil Society on the Body Politic of Cameroon

The relationship between civil society and democracy is a complex one, and the emergence of a civil society does not guarantee the development of democracy however it is highly unlikely that a viable democracy can survive without a civil society, because civil society is a necessary foundation for democracy (Woods 1992). It is within civil society that public opinion is formed and it is through independent associations that individuals can have some influence on government decision-making. Despite the fact that the Cameroon civil society had a bearing on at least the democratization of the state, some African scholars have represented civil society as weak and unable to perform any effective role in promoting democracy

(Bratton 1989) The Cameroon example has however shown the contrary. The movement from a monolithic one-party system to a multi-party system was one of the first fruits of tree of civil society in Cameroon. In December 1990, after considerable pressure on the government, a series of laws to liberalise Cameroon's political landscape were promulgated. In the same year the University of Yaounde, the lone university in the country, was decentralised, and the Buea and Ngaoundere campuses were transformed into full-fledged universities. In a related vein the General Certificate of Education Board was created in 1993.

Cameroon has undergone four major elections since then—1992, 1997, 2002 and presidential elections in 2004—but after all these elec-tions there has been general disenchantment with the electoral process due to massive rigging, non-registration of voters, low participation, unfulfilled promises and sterile political debates between the ruling party, the Cameroon's People Democratic Movement (CPDM), and the opposition parties. Despite these shortcomings one cannot deny that these elections came about largely as a result of pressure from the civil society in Cameroon since the 1990s. To be sure the civil society itself had shortcomings, firstly because it was led by human beings, some of whom only wanted to satisfy their bellies, but also because the government was unwilling to give up power. The next section of this paper will examine the flaws of civil society in Cameroon in the 1990s.

## Drawbacks of Civil Society in Cameroon

Whatever we say about civil society in Cameroon in the 1990s, it should be borne in mind that it was neither homogenous nor wholly emancipatory. In fact civil society was contradictory, exhibiting both democratic and despotic tendencies (Fatton; 1995; Chabal 1994). The lack of homogeneity in the civil society in Cameroon can easily be explained on the basis of ethnicity. Cameroon is made up of approximately 240 ethnic groups (Takougang and Krieger 1998; Yenshu 2001), which helps keep civil society weak, as different indigenous groups and individuals pursue their own agendas (Bayart 1993). Moreover individuals belonging to elites were even given the go-ahead by the ruling regime to form ethnic associations to counter the opposition (Nyamnjoh and Michael 1998).

The pitfalls of civil society can also be explained by the role of the government. It is difficult for Cameroon to evolve a viable, inclusive and participatory governance structure due to its long history of autocratic rule, but this difficulty has been increased by the state's use of political stratagems such as divide-and-rule, prebendalism, patronage and clientelism, all of which have led to the informalisation of politics (Mbuagbo and Akoko, 2004; Bayart 1993; Konings 2002; Nyamnjoh 1999). Through these methods the ruling government has penetrated civil society and survived by 'buying off sections of the civil society.

This happens because of mediocrity in leadership. Therefore, to achieve a sustainable and vibrant civil society in Cameroon, human resources development or capacity-building must be rekindled and kept alive (Forje 2003). Given the ideological individualism and the fear of subordinate classes, the elite individuals in civil society are prone to all sorts of opportunistic defections and personal accommodations with the authorities. The defections of Ahmadu Vamoulke to become the General Manager of Cameroon Radio and Television (CRTV) and a central committee member and of Bello Bouba Maigari to the camp of CPDM are classic cases in point (Nyamnjoh 1999). Thus individuals or groups within civil society were appeased or rewarded in order for rulers to stay in power. Coercion itself is expensive; the armed forces, police, paramilitary and presidential guard must all be satisfied if they are not to take power themselves (Chabal 1994). All these factors have rendered civil society weak in Cameroon.

In addition university professors, teachers, tutors and rectors are disorganized and fragmented, preferring to accept sinecures and pursue narrow ethnic agendas rather than fight for their professional interests. With civil society divided amongst itself, the dynamic civil society of the 1990s has become a mirage fifteen years later. Today civil society in Cameroon has collapsed for a variety of reasons ranging from regionalism to the political acrobatics of the state. Non-governmental organizations have sprouted like mushrooms, but many exist only in suitcases and their leaders have no iota of civic responsibility. At this juncture, what can be done to enable civil society in Cameroon to play its desired role?

## Which Way Forward?

This part of the chapter attempts to suggest the way forward towards a viable, vibrant civil society in Cameroon. Although Cameroonian scholars such as Awasom (2005), Forje (2003), and Nyamnjoh (1999) have attempted to provide such a way forward for civil society in Cameroon, a concrete programme has not been adequately developed. My suggestions will therefore be specific to the Cameroon situation rather than globalised, although global paradigms will be borrowed when necessary. For close to fifteen years the civil society in Cameroon has remained in a morass, bespattered with societal cleavages which find expression in tendencies ranging from ethnicism to regionalism, thereby limiting its ability to mobilise the masses towards a meaningful democratic space.

The way out of this dismal situation requires civil society to tran-scend narrow, social and political boundaries and identify with the daily and legitimate struggles of ordinary citizens. Nyamnjoh (1999) argues that attempts to empower civil society in Cameroon have met with little success because of poor organisation, while Yenshu (2001) blames weak social mobilisation in a context of repressive laws that stifle real political and social debates. To overcome these problems civil society in Cameroon must therefore develop its capacity through a national network capable of developing a more consistent and coherent democratic discourse and of promoting practices and attitudes that defend the fundamental rights of citizens. This requires a synergy among the various elements of civil society to bring pressure to bear on all anti-democratic forces in the state. The experience in many other African countries, especially in South Africa, could be emulated in Cameroon. The contributions of mass political mobilisation and awareness-building among civil society organizations to achieve social transformation in South Africa should serve as an inspiration to budding civil society organizations in Cameroon (Orkin 1995).

The idea of civil society is not new, but what would appear to be new is its organization within the modern state and its presupposition of a global character. According to De Oliveira and Tandon (1994) human beings have always come together for a common cause, and the gregarious nature of humankind is expressed in an associational life of diverse character and objectives. This diverse character, according to Bayart (1993), should include villagers, fishermen, nomads, members of different age groups, village councillors, slum dwellers and all others who are, or feel they are, without due access to state resources, as well as professionals, politicians, priest and mullahs, intellectuals, military officers. This human solidarity, with its historic and philosophical origins, is known as civil society and nowadays in Cameroon requires greater citizen participation and influence in the affairs of modern states than ever before.

Today there is empirical evidence of the existence of a plethora of movements in Cameroon within civil society, but most of these are in towns and cities. The most notorious of these movements are the NGOs. These NGOs are not only limited to towns and cities, but some do not even have offices. They exist in suitcases. Their limitation is also dictated by the fact that those who fund them dictate what they should do. Because of this, the interest of the masses is not reflected. Civil society deals with transforming the society; it therefore goes without saying that they must be built up from community levels and operates throughout the country. The mass of Cameroon's people live in the countryside; they need to be integrated into the new political culture and organized and educated through a bottom-up approach.

Civil society in Cameroon is anaemic and fractured. Mkandawire and Olukoshi (1995) maintain that a strong civil society is characterised by the existence of well-organized, highly elaborated, autonomous and self-conscious institutions and associational activities. These may be trade unions, religious or professional associations or traditional authorities, etc. In Zambia, for example, the politically effective characteristics of civil society are modern, while in Nigeria traditional power structures combine with modern ones to create a highly differentiated and articulate civil society.

Current approaches in civil society represent the so-called neo-liberal explanations of social realities that have neo-colonial undertones. Richard Joseph (1978) aptly captures this as an 'ideological facade' designed to distract from a thorough empirical and theoretical explanation of Africa's social realities. Civil society in Cameroon has been stigmatised and asphyxiated since the postcolonial period (Gifford 1997). Today the Cameroon state, although a collapsed one, should take up its responsibility to empower and strengthen civil society. Some states are beginning to see the wisdom of strengthening civil society so that people's interests can be articulated effectively. For example Sierra Leone has been engaged in civil awareness programmes aimed at sensitizing citizens about their civic rights. More needs to be done in this direction in Cameroon, and there is also a need to mount massive political awareness campaigns in order to sensitise both the state and civil society about their roles and responsibilities (Ceesay 1998). Cameroon could also go further to nurture a culture of tolerance, debate and accommodation in order to overcome the dangers of ethnic attachments. This can be achieved if specially trained people are employed to educate civil society groups in both urban and rural areas.

Osaghae (1998) maintains that the neoliberal view pitches civil society as alternative, and even opposed to the state. This neo-liberal conceptualisation evolved and has been popularised within a narrowly defined ideological and historical moment, one which sees civil society as the spearhead and defender of economic and political liberalisation. In the same vein Mbuagbo and Robert (2004) maintains that a Eurocentric and unilinear perspective on civil society, like other development-oriented concepts, is not warranted by historical evidence. Mamdani (1995) argues that we are faced with the problem of viewing social phenomena out of context and imposing explanations not derived from empirical observations of actual social processes but by analogy from antecedent but different historical occurrences. In line with Mamdani this paper proposes autocentric research towards the understanding of civil society in Cameroon. This research should be long term and thoroughly grounded on methodology. Fundamental research should be conducted to come up with viable governance that will anchor the aspirations of the people. Today the Chinese are a challenge to the West because they took time in fundamental research. Research organisations such as the Council for the Development of Social Science Research in Africa (CODESRIA) should start funding meaningful research projects on civil society in Cameroon. The research should be manned by people with a high moral and intellectual reputation, since Cameroon has been named twice as the most corrupt country in the world.

To locate the role of civil society in the present political process in Cameroon is like searching for a pin in a haystack. Civil society has been paralysed by ethnic cleavages. The political liberalisation in Cameroon since 1990 has exposed dormant feelings of ethnic animosity, while pro-government vigilante groups emerged for various political reasons to counter the alliance between the minority Anglophones and Bamileke ethnic group that threatened to rob the ruling clique and their supporters of their political privileges (Konings 2002; Mbuagbo and Robert 2004). These ethnic fissures must be resolved and questions around citizenship and voting rights must not preoccupy the political agenda.

There is no doubt that civil society in Africa in general and Cameroon in particular is threatened by the particularism of ethnicity and other atomistic tendencies (Woods 1992). A fully developed civil society in Cameroon should help create norms that would limit the character of ethnic and cultural particularism. It is unlikely, however, that a civil society will develop in Cameroon that is completely void of ethnic tensions and divisions, but structures can be created to contain the problem. Civil society in Cameroon should be questioning its own raison d'être like other human institutions. By cross-examining itself, it will know whether it is worthwhile. The growth of civil society requires organizational development to enable leaders to exercise influence over government on behalf of their members. When this type of institution-allocation exists, even authoritarian regimes such as the one in apartheid South Africa have to give grudging recognition to the civil society (Sklar 1987).

## Conclusion

Civil society in Cameroon has failed to achieve its most important goal—societal transformation. The reasons range from ethnicism to regionalism to elitism. The failure of the government to introduce democratic reforms is seen everywhere—from widespread abuses of human rights to the most blatant forms of corruption. These problems further inhibit the effectiveness of civil society in Cameroon in bringing meaningful change. To rescue itself from this banalised mire, civil society must transcends narrow ethnic, social and political boundaries and embrace the daily and legitimate struggles of ordinary citizens. This is the only way to move towards meaningful quantitative and qualitative development. Our next focus will be on football, "the one time opium of Cameroon".

# Chapter Eight

## Football and the Politics of Belonging in Contemporary Cameroon, C.1979-2004: A Historical Meditation

### Introduction

Sports are a physical outdoor activity for exercise and amusement, usually played in a specific area and according to fixed rules. This includes hockey, volleyball, cricket, football, tennis, jumping, and running. In Cameroon, football has become 'the opium of the people' since 1990 when she became the first African country ever to reach the quarter finals of the World Cup fiesta. She subsequently participated in the 1994, 1998 and 2002 World Cup competitions, but never went beyond the 16th finals. In Africa, Cameroon has won the Cup of Nations four times. This paper critically examines why and how football has gone beyond the sporting activity for mere leisure in Cameroon and has become a political tool in the hands of the government within the ongoing debate of ethnic loyalties and the politics of belonging. The author uses mainly primary/secondary sources and personal experiences to defend the position that it is not enough to play football in Cameroon, but what matters more is one's ethnic background and how a competition in which Cameroon is involved is used by political stalwarts to moderate the political climate at home.

### Background

On the 8th of July 1979, the Public Works Department (PWD) Football Social Club of Bamenda clashed with Canon Football Social Club of Yaoundé while the Dynamo Football Social Club clashed with Union Abong Mbang Football Social Club in a semi final Cup of Cameroon encounter. The PWD Football Club defeated Canon while Dynamo humbled Union Abong Mbang. The final of the Cup of Cameroon was *ipso facto* between PWD Bamenda, an Anglophone club against Dynamo Douala, a Francophone club and ethnically a Bassa based club. The PWD club had fought very hard by eliminating very prestigious football clubs in the 16th finals, quarter and semi finals. PWD crushed Etoile Filante Club of Garoua from the home town of President Ahmadou Ahidjo by seven goals to zero during the 16th finals; humbled Tonnere Football Club, a very prestigious club from Yaoundé by one goal to zero in the quarter finals. During the semi-finals PWD beat Canon which was the most powerful team of the day by one goal to zero to qualify for the finals (*Cameroon Times*, 1979).

The entire width and breadth of the Anglophone territory galvanised and expected nothing less than grasping the trophy for the first time. Unfortunately, it was rumoured that Epese, a defender of PWD and a Bassa by ethnic origin was contacted by the Minister of Youths and Sports, Felix Tonye Mbock and the officials of the Dynamo squad to betray the PWD team during the finals by giving him a juicy parcel. During the match, the rumour continued, Epese intentionally jump into the air and instead of heading the ball out of the 5.5m box, he caught the ball with the hand. This was repeatedly done three times and all these times resulted in penalty kicks. The entire penalty kicks resulted in goals and at the end of the day, Dynamo defeated PWD by three goals to one. Epese who had been a good defender was held responsible for the lost finals. This rumour was confirmed by the ex-goalkeeper of PWD, (Agwa, Personal communication, 14 March 2006; Group discussion, 10 February 2007).

From ethnographic data gathered in the field so far, Epese betrayed the team because he had no ethnic affiliation to either Bamenda or any of the Anglophone regions. If that is true, it was therefore a matter of belonging and not just playing football. However, President Ahidjo grudgingly handed over the trophy and set up a commission of enquiry to investigate what happened with the Cup of Cameroon finals that PWD had to lose the way it did. The results of the commission did not proof the contrary. Ahidjo, therefore responded by sacking the Minister of Youths and Sport for working in complicity with Epese to betray justice (Personal communication with Zachary Nkwo, 10-15 October 2006 and 15-30 February 2007). One might wonder aloud why the President had to set up a commission of enquiry. The plausible reason was that he wanted to use the cup as a political ploy since his most cherished dream was to forge national unity. The part of the country which seemed to have been in the minority, West Cameroon was to make it feel part and parcel of the nation by honourably handing over the cup to it. Of course, it had proved that it could win the cup. On the other hand, Dynamo too had proven that it could also win the cup. The bottom line is that President Ahidjo wanted to use the cup for cosmetic politics in building the nation.

When the finals of the Cup of Cameroon was played in 2000 between Kumbo Strikers and Sable Batie, Kumbo Strikers grasped the Cup of Cameroon and for its first time the cup "spoke and understood" the English language. In certain quarters, the cup has thus become bilingual. After the cup finals on Sunday 17 December 2000, the players and the team officials took the cup to the Prime Minister's residence who was an Anglophone from the South West Province. By taking the cup to the Prime Minister, one can quickly guess rightly or wrongly that it was the issue of identity and belonging because it might have been impossible to take the cup to the Prime Minister, if he was a Francophone. The Prime Minister, however, did not fail to romance the cup with the politics of the day. In his speech which was broadcasted over the Television several times, the Prime Minister said *inter alia:* that football in Cameroon is a very strong unifier and that the cup will be used for democracy. He ended up by saying that the team took the cup from the President's hand which was a very big honour and many people saw the players shaking hands with the president. On Tuesday 19 December 2000, the players and team officials took the cup and crossed the Mungo River into the South West Province. It was then presented to the Mayor of the Buea Rural Council, Endeley who spoke in the same lines with the Prime Minister. According to him, football means oneness and symbolised national unity. Supporters alike saw the crossing of the cup over the waters of the River Mungo as cementing the unity of Cameroon.

All the speeches and actions made in relation to the Cup of Cameroon by government officials cannot be taken uncritically vis-à-vis our pith and kernel of the discourse in this chapter. As already said, the action of Epese showed in no small way that it was not enough to play football in Cameroon but more where the player comes from. Secondly, the Prime Minister spoke of football as a unifier because since 1960 when Cameroon gained independence, the search for unity like in most African countries has been the dream of most political leaders who hold the reign of power although all seemed to be ending up in an illusion. The case of Cameroon is no exception. Evidence shows that it is not only the politics of belonging which has been at the root cause of national unity being an illusion but many factors seem to have played a role either indirectly or directly. Most Cameroonians and in particular the Anglophones felt that they had always been disenfranchised during elections in the multi-party era. The first democratic elections took place in Cameroon in 1992.

It came on the heels of tension that had just passed in 1990 when multi party politics was introduced and at a time when the national team was causing sensation and fascination in the World Cup Finals in Milan, Italy by first humbling the cup holders, Argentina, current World Cup champions by one goal to zero. The Indomitable Lions went ahead to qualify for the quarter finals thereby making nonsense of the white superiority over football. Political activism died down as the national team scored victories in the World Cup and Cameroonians thought and acted as a nation. However, the use of the word unifier here may also mean the political divide that had existed between the North westerners and South westerners since the days of nationalism in the 1960s (Gam Nkwi, 2006). Football, therefore, was seen as glue which could paper the political cracks in Cameroon.

In any case, all was political rhetoric. During the 2005 Interpools Competition (a competition of ten teams which is played to select the best three into elite division one) which lasted from November to December, 2005 in Buea and Douala, the North West representative in this competition was the Yong Sports Academy (YOSA). In their opening match, YOSA trounced their opponents by four goals to one. That sent a chill down the spines of any team that was to meet YOSA. As the competition progressed, it became clearer that the team could not follow up her victories and one of the lame reasons was that there were many Francophones in the team. It was again rumoured that they were bought over by the officials of the other teams by promising and paying much money for any match that they had to lose. That promise heightened their losing spirits. This implied that the team was going to be knocked out prematurely even before the competition comes to an end. If that was to be the case which indeed it was, the only two Anglophone teams that remained to vie for a division 1 ticket were Mount Cameroon Football Club and Kumba Lakers Football Club. The fixtures for the last playing day pitted YOSA versus Kumba Lakers and Mount Cameroon versus Federal Foumban. The Kumba Lakers needed a victory which YOSA did not hesitate to give because there were no stakes facing them and Mount Cameroon needed just a draw for the Kumba Lakers to qualify for the next round of the competition. The outcome of this rigmarole was determined on an ethnic chessboard. The founder and managing director of Mount Cameroon was a Francophone from the Western Region, Calvin Faounding and Federal Foumban was still from the Western Region, a few kilometres from Bafoussam the home of the Director of Mount Cameroon. Secondly it was the base of the Sultan, the most powerful traditional ruler in Central Cameroon. The managing director did everything for the team from Foumban to beat his team, Mount Cameroon. That strategy worked out as he planned and at the end of the day Federal Foumban which by merit would never have gone to division one, qualified and Kumba Lakers packed bag and baggage home to Division 2. The South westerners as well as other Anglophones cried out aloud for such a thing to happen. As if that was not enough, Faounding went ahead to make arrangements with the already corrupted FECAFOOT that the Mount Cameroon team will be playing her matches but in Douala. Perhaps, this was speculated on the backdrop that the team was going to lose support from the Southwest indigenous population. It is obvious from the foregoing discussions that the director of Mount Cameroon football team had done what he did because he was a francophone. To add to that the chemistry of 80 percent of the players in the team were Francophones. Furthermore, it shows that it is not enough to play football in Cameroon but rather it is enough to know where a player belongs before playing in a particular team or where a team president/manager comes from before owning a team.

In January 2007, Mount Cameroon was suddenly dumped to Division 3 on grounds of match fixing and some of its officials banned for ten years never to participate in any football activity in Cameroon (*The Post*, 2007). The then General Manager of

FECAFOOT (Cameroon Football Federation), Jean Lambert Nang signed and issued a communiqué to this effect and justified his "rash" decision so to say, on grounds that there was a match fixing between Racing Club of Bafoussam, ( the hometown of the Managing Director of Mount Cameroon) and Mount Cameroon Football Club. At the close of the 2005/2006 division1 football season in Cameroon, Impot Football Club of Yaoundé, (the hometown of the General Manager of FECAFOOT, had filed a complaint to the Disciplinary and Homologation Committee of FECAFOOT, accusing Mount Cameroon Football Club and Racing Football Club for match fixing in their last encounter which took place in Bafoussam (*The Post*, 2007). If Mount Cameroon was relegated then *Impot* Football Club would be restored to Division 1. The General Manager, first acting on the basis of prerogatives vested on him and secondly that he hailed from Yaoundé where the ailing team came from, unilaterally decided to sign the obnoxious decree sending Mount Cameroon not only to Division 2 but to Division 3 which is most peripheral in Cameroon Football landscape.

This chapter draws its inspiration from the above snapshots and gets into the pith and kernel of the paper which is to examine politics, football and politics of belonging in contemporary Cameroon. No doubt football like other issues has received much scholarly attention recently in Africa in general and Cameroon in particular. Vidacs (2006:331-349) attempts to interrogate why Africanists study sports in general and football in particular. Schatzberg (2006:351-369) and Pelak (2006:371-392), links global processes, democratisation and women's football in South Africa. Lekunze (2006) examines an insight into the unending intrigues, fraud, treachery, mismanagement, corruption, segregation, unfair trials and tribulations that African football has suffered over the years on the World soccer chessboard. Scholars have also researched and written about football in Cameroon from multifarious perspectives. Some have written about the origin of football and those who were the first people to introduce it (Tanga, 1969:45). Others have written about the "operation coup de coeur" a voluntary financial donation made by Cameroonians of good will to rescue their team from financial quagmire during the 1994 World Cup jamboree in the United States of America (Nkwi and Vidacs,1997).Others still have written about the evolution of football in Cameroon in what they have preferred to term "Modernisation and Football in Cameroon" (Clignet and Stark, 1974).Yet others have treated football in Cameroon in relationship to the African continent and specifically treated what national teams like the Indomitable Lions of Cameroon, the Teranga Lions of Senegal and Green Eagles of Nigeria symbolise to the Nation and its people (Mehler, 2002:12-13).Yet, others have treated football and politics as in Cameroon (Nkwi and Vidacs,1997). Others have treated Football and Identity in Cameroon and football and anti-colonial sentiment in Cameroon (Vidacs, 2003:167-184; 1997). Pannenborg, (2008:198) handles the football phenomenon in Cameroon from an anthropological perspective and concludes that in Cameroon, "It is evident that football is closely linked to both economics and politics. At both local and national levels, tribalism is working full force: football is an arena in which the country's different ethnic groups are struggling to gain power and dominance in a relatively non-violent manner".

Drawing from the literature above, it shows that football and the politics of belonging has not been given adequate treatment. It has been at best partially handled. It has not been given a central stage in research. This is obviously a hiatus which this present chapter hopes to fill. Nonetheless the views expressed by the above scholars will not be discarded *in toto* but some of the paradigms will be used in the present work. On the backdrop of the lacunae, the chapter attempts to unravel how and why football has gone beyond the normal sporting activity of mere leisure in Cameroon and has become a political tool in the hands of the government within the ongoing debate of ethnic loyalties and politics of belonging.

## The Notion of Politics of Belonging

In 1990, many parts of Africa South of the Sahara embraced a new political dynamics. There was an unprecedented drive towards political and economic liberalization, including threats to evict most African dictators, sparked by a general call for democratization and the consequent rebirth of multi-party politics. Political kleptocrats responded by engendering and intensifying the struggle over belonging and forms of exclusion among their citizens. Some were branded "natives" while others were called "strangers", even if they were citizens of the same country. Even children of the same family were declared born out of wedlock and therefore did not belong to the family. Although this undermined the very notion of national citizenship, which most regimes in Africa had upheld in the early 1960s and 1970s, using unity as a precondition for nation building (Geschiere, 2004), these same authoritarian regimes began encouraging conflict between indigenous groups and strangers in order to remain in power. In Cameroon in particular, the ruling government since 1990, under President Paul Biya, placed additional emphasis on the invention of new forms of ethnicity and the political fungi of belonging have been given a sharp fillip. This strategy was meant to enhance the divide and rule system and stay in power (Gam Nkwi, 2006:123-143). However, the literature on the politics of belonging tends to give the impression that it was only in the 1990s that it actually began (Geschiere, 2000; Geschiere and Nyamnjoh, 1999; Nyamnjoh and Rowlands, 1998:320-337; Oben and Akoko, 2004: 241-258; Mamdani, 1996). Either by accident or by design, the politics of belonging started romancing with football sometimes in the late 1970s. This paper is meant to give a new twist by contributing to the mainstream debate of the politics of belonging with focus on football in Cameroon. This combination has not been hitherto handled in Cameroonian scholarship.

## The Methodology of Data Collection

The ethnographic data for the paper were gotten through discussions with some of the actors and actresses as well as observers and football fans who had lived through the experiences. We started by falling in love with the topic and then proceeded to discussing it with people who were interesting to listen to us talk and share their own versions of the story. From that type of method, we quickly got to know people who lived through the experiences. We made appointments with the people and met with them for several hours in both their houses and offices. That method was quite fruitful given that we allowed the informants to talk as much as they could before we proceeded to ask leading questions. During the discussions, some of the informants like Zachary Nkwo and Ni Sam Nuvala Fonkem proved to be more knowledgeable than us in several aspects and did help us to reshape our ideas and the paper in general. We then proceeded to the archives where we found that the *West Cameroon Champion* newspaper and *Cameroon Times* were carrying very relevant information. We then crosschecked the archival material with the empirical data which we had collected. We then realised that it was imperative for us to get to reading relevant secondary data. In August 2003, we acquired the first secondary data from the Council for the Development of Social Science Research in Africa (CODESRIA). At the Afrika Studie Centrum in Leiden, The Netherlands, we had access to most of the relevant data on football. The latest publication on football in Cameroon was made available to us by our promoter, Prof. Dr. Mirjam Elizabeth de Bruijn. The methodology employed in this paper therefore is a combination of primary and secondary sources.

## Birth and Attempts at Politicising Football in Cameroon

According to Tanga, (1969) football was first introduced in Cameroon in its economic capital, Douala, around the 1920s by the African migrants. These migrants who were already assimilated thought that they were closer to the Europeans and so attempted to exclude the indigenous people from playing against them or playing with them. If this was true then the politics of fooballisation had started by the very fact that there was already exclusion. The city of Douala first, and Yaounde which was the second city for football to be introduced remained for a very long time the hub of the earliest teams, perhaps because they were the strong holds of French colonial administration (Vidacs, 2004:171). Recent studies point to the fact that the centres of football have been changing to other provinces like the West Province. Clignet and Stark (2004:56) maintain that there was a time when some of the teams recruited players strictly on ethnic lines although in the mid 1970s and most recently the trend has changed. Players, coaches are more mobile but the overall support of the teams is from the ethnic base. At what point in time and with what ramifications were players recruited on ethnic lines? Which were those teams that recruited players on ethnic lines? Clignet and Stark have not addressed these critical issues.

In the present day Southwest and Northwest Regions which were under British Mandate and Trusteeship colonial administration, between 1919 and 1961, the history of football appeared to be quite different. Football was introduced later than in the francophone zone of the country, and the infant teams were mainly sponsored by corporations and governmental agencies. The Public Works Department owned teams in both provinces known as PWD Football Social Club based in Kumba, Bamenda, Victoria and Mamfe. These were administrative head quarters in the British Southern Cameroons often known as the Cameroons Province. Amongst these teams, PWD Bamenda reached the finals of the Cup of Cameroon in 1979 although it lost it (*Cameroon Times*, 1979). The Cameroon Electric Corporation also had a team known as POWERCAM. Generally, football started in Cameroon as a francophone affair and for a very long time the Anglophones remained at the margins of that sport. Their marginalisation never went on *sine die* as some of their teams climbed to the finals of the Cameroon cup. A case in point was PWD Bamenda which played but lost the cup in 1979 as already mentioned. The Francophones saw themselves as owners of football in Cameroon. In 1990 when the Lions were hopping from victory, to victory one could hear Francophones say *"même les anglo sont content"* meaning that even the Anglophones were satisfied with the victories even if the team was captained by an Anglophone, Stephen Tataw. This was a cynical way of saying that the Anglophones should not have sentiments when it comes to football.

This type of barren reasoning points to, and gives the impression that football belongs to only the Francophone rightly or wrongly. The creation of the Cameroon Football Federation (FECAFOOT) in 1959, just one year to independence was to illustrate this fact more eloquently. The overall body charged with the organisation of football in Cameroon has been FECAFOOT. The organigram shows that since its inception no Anglophone has ever been the president. Instead, the Francophones have dominated the FECAFOOT just like they have done by ruling Cameroon since the departure of the French colonial masters. Even those who deputise the president border on what one could call powder-face Anglophones. The politics that bedevils FECAFOOT is analogous to the politics of the state. At one time the president of FECAFOOT is from the Centre, where the president of the Republic hails from and at another time he is from the North where the first president, a Fulani came from. Since independence, power at the presidency has radiated and swung between the north and south so with FECAFOOT.

If football and the politics of belonging were anything to go by, FECAFOOT is a better illustration. Out of a total work force of more than three hundred in her headquarters; two hundred and fifty are Francophones. The Francophones whose numerical strength is also great in the country, at least with a ratio of 5:2 control the reins football. They are those who remote-controlled referee to award matches to their favourite teams. This explains why two teams will lock horns in a football encounter and all of them will emerge victorious. This also explains why 80 percent of Interpool competitions which are usually organised to select the first best three teams to join the elite division have remained largely a francophone affair. Most of the  football seasons like 2007, the entire Anglophone zone has only one Division 1, Mount Cameroon Football Club, which FECAFOOT has threatened in the beginning of the football season, that all her  football matches will be played in Douala, 45 minutes drive from Buea and situated in the francophone zone. All these point to the politicisation of football in Cameroon by its highest organ, FECAFOOT. Because the leadership of the association is over concentrated on one ethnic group by 1994 it was riddled by leadership problems rather than seeing into the *bene esse* of the football in the country, especially the national team. There was a conflict of authority between the president and the Minister of Youths and Sports, Bernard Massuoa. Later, it was a confrontation between a majority of the football organisation's Central Committee and the then President, Paschal Owona (*Cameroon Tribune*, 1994). When the president finally left total confusion stepped in and it was only with the intervention of the government that things returned to normal. Personal experiences and discussions with people who had been active in football in Cameroon add more weight to the politics of belonging to this football loving nation.

The decision that Mount Cameroon football club will play her matches in Douala was a bitter pill for the Anglophones and the team officials to swallow. Chrysantus Nkongso and Gordon Nwambo Ngu, Vice President and legal adviser of Mount Cameroon football club respectively, crumbled under the cruel weight of the FECAFOOT sledgehammer and were suspended from all FECAFOOT activities for a period of ten years. Nkongso, while reacting to the FECAFOOT decision, said that it was unjust and called on the population of the South West and Buea in particular to remain calm and that the matter was under control (*The Post*, 2007). The ding dong of the FECAFOOT's manager rocked on until the heavy pen of the Prime Minister fell and the decision was technically reversed. The Prime Minister stated unequivocally that the 16-team-league-system should be adopted instead of the 18-team-league system adopted by the latter for the 2007 Division 1 football season. Although the decision of the Prime Minister lay to rest the whole controversy, it drove home yet another lesson to be learnt from football in Cameroon. There is no gainsaying that the Prime Minister's intervention was pegged on the fact that he comes from the South West where the impact of the FECAFOOT's manager was most felt and for the general interest of the Anglophone community which was to go without any first division. On top of all the politics and belonging that has characterised the Cameroonian football since its inception, it is imperative that we examine the Indomitable Lions. The next section of the paper now turns to the Indomitable Lions or *les Lions Indomptables*

## Indomitable Lions

The appellation Indomitable Lions was derived from the conquering prowess in the early 1970s. This team had its first qualification for a World Cup Tournament in 1982. While in Spain, the team created record by being the only team that emerged from that competition without conceding a defeat and above all from Africa. The name remained and almost a decade passed by without the team making any headway out of Africa. In 1990, it qualified for the 1990 World Cup fiesta in Italy and started off by beating the defending champions; Argentina in Milan on June 30th, 1990 after two of their players had been expelled from the field of play with red cards. This victory was followed up till the quarter finals when the Indomitable Lions were unjustifiably bundled out in their match with England. Spectators stayed on in the field after the match and watched the Lions run round the field while waving at the crowd. Two things could be driven home from the two competitions.

The first one is that in 1982, the composition of the team was made up of Francophones and the country at the time was politically stable. One could not hear anything about the politics of belonging but it was however simmering in the team. The second is that the World Cup coincided in 1990 with political activism in Cameroon-the re-birth of multi-party politics. The first opposition political party, the Social Democratic Front (SDF) was formed in Bamenda, on 26th May 1990 amidst opposition from the government. With the birth of this party in the Anglophone zone the ruling regime saw the Anglophones as the enemy of the state. The state was at the verge of collapsing. The first victory of the Lions downplayed the political tension that was existing in Cameroon and above all the President was in the field at Milan and TV cameras had to focus on him several times when he was clapping and cheering the team. There were two Anglophones in the team and one was the captain. From 1990, the Lions subsequently participated at the 1994, 1998, 2002 World Cup competitions and interspersed their appearance by winning the African Cup of Nations several times. The team went as far as playing the Confederation Cup finals in 2002.

The Lions, therefore, from all these victories have remained a symbol of national unity although at the same time, the ethnic composition of the team has remained a political issue (Mehler, 2002:12). Either the team's 75 percent is Bassa ethnic group based or Beti. Although Cameroon was quickly eliminated at the 2002 World Cup as at that year she remained the best African country following FIFA rankings. According to Mehler (2002:13) "After two championships in a row (2000 and 2002 as well as 1984 and 1988, the Olympic Gold Medal (in 2000) and qualification for the World Cup in 1982, 1990, 1994, 1998 and 2002 Cameroon was undisputed Number 1 of African soccer before the tournament. The early elimination of the Indomitable Lions in 2002 put those successes in perspectives". These victories were closely followed up by the regime which failed to supply genuine democracy to the *hoi polloi*. It therefore hides under the cloak of football to make political gains.

Most of the time when the lions win a trophy the next day is declared a public holiday and the trophy is taken round the main cities of the country. At one time the coach is seated in a military jeep while a motorcade follows the cup. When the team won the

2000 Gold Medal in Sydney, it passed through Paris to play a friendly football match with the French National team. In 2002, the team was admitted into the presidency to shake hands with the presidential couple and medals were awarded to the players. The photo below shows the Indomitable Lions with the President of the Republic and his wife after being decorated. They had successfully come home with the trophy and thus it was a cause for celebration. The honour to them was to admit them into the Presidency while the President and his wife congratulated the players and decorated them.

Apart from entering the Presidency and shaking hands with the Presidential couple, sometimes, the presidential couple sent food and cooks to the lions like in Mali 2002 and Ghana 2008. All these points to the fact that football and politics have become synonymous in Cameroon. The admission of the team into the presidency is perhaps a cosmetic sign of a failed state. The only option to a state in which all other organs have failed can only depend on victory to pretend that all is going on well. The team ought to pass through France after winning a goal medal in 2000, to show the world that France was and is still her colonial master. Most of the political predicaments that have bedevilled Cameroon have been blamed on France. Yet, a football trophy stands the chance of blinding the blames.

That notwithstanding, the meaning of Indomitable Lions has evolved with astonishing ambiguity. Nyamnjoh (2005:153) aptly captures these meanings in the political context of Cameroon. According to him

As recently as July 2000, one could hear the manager of CRTV, Professor Gervais Mendo Ze, who has been general manager of CRTV for over fourteen years and has masterminded most of the manipulation that have kept President Paul Biya recycling mediocrity and perfecting the insensitivities of illegitimate power, boasting that the CRTV journalists were Les Lions Indomptables de l'audio visuel. At the 1992 presidential elections, Paul Biya had presented himself as l'homme Lion, imbued with the power, courage and intension of protecting Cameroon from Les marchands d'illusions, of whom John Fru Ndi and his SDF were presented as champions by the CRTV. In taxis, beer parlours, chicken parlours and elsewhere, Biya's message was seen by ordinary people as a

*The National Team players, the coach, Minister of Youth and Sports, the President of FECAFOOT and the technical crew at the Presidency after winning the 2002 African Cup of Nations*

corruption of reality. He was a Lion no doubt, but his mission was not to safe. Rather, he was asking for five more years to accomplish his devastation of Cameroon and Cameroonians. Such alternative interpretations never made their way onto CRTV, not even though the other presidential candidates whose campaign broadcast were heavily monitored and censored. Jean Jacque Ekindi, for example, as foremost chasseur du Lion, would have his trenchant campaign counter offensives banned by CRTV management. Cameroon in short had space only for three Indomitable Lions: President Biya, the CRTV and the national team, whose victories fame the president and CRTV caricature through manipulation and corruption. This guarantees that the indomitable lion of politics shall appropriate the victories and fame of the indomitable lions of football thanks to the facilitation and manipulation by the indomitable lion of broadcasting. It makes it possible for government to feed the people not with the facts but with the options only, so that they cannot and never should think for themselves. Truth, the indomitable lion of politics (Biya) has never tired of affirming, comes from above and rumour from below (la vérité vient d'en haut, la rumuer vient d'en bas). By regularly feeding the public with falsehood and denying the opposition forces the opportunity to demonstrate otherwise, the CPDM government has attempted for over two decades to persuade the public that it should take its world of appearances as the true reality. There is neither corruption nor embezzlement-repeated reports by Transparency International and also by nationals notwithstanding State television portrays only a safe less effort at nation building by a benevolent President Biya, his ministers, directors and bureaucrats. Tribalism, Nepotism, and inequalities do not exist, only national unity, balanced regional development and the equitable distribution of the national cake. Documented evidence to the contrary is simply brushed aside as coming from people of bad faith who are blind to the merits and achievements of the indomitable lion of politics who has made Cameroon the pride of Africa.

The name Indomitable Lions which used to be the name of the national team has been appropriated by Biya and Mendo Ze, all from the Beti ethnic group which is the dominant ethnic group in the Centre Province. If these people have shown recently that the Lion belonged to them, the Cameroonians appeared to have shown the contrary in 1994 during the World Cup competition in the U.S.A. The regime which had taken up the symbol of the Lion and always shielding the reality hatched a plot in 1994 that the national team was facing financial problems in the U.S and therefore it was opening a fund for financial voluntary contribution from the public. This plot was obviously to ravage even the widow's mite that was left in the pockets of the masses. This fund was code-named "*operation coup du couer*" which might simply means a gift from the heart.

The *operation coup du couer,* was therefore, launched at the end of June 1994 to financially support the indomitable lions. The reaction of the public was spontaneous and Cameroonians of all works of life contributed (children, adults, men and even the blind contributed). One of the main reasons for the massive contribution was because the shadows of victory of 1990 Italia was still fresh in the memories of Cameroonians. It was, therefore, felt that the victories of Italy will continue and go even beyond. Such great expectations were to show total disappointment both to the Cameroon public and the Lions. Their first match with Sweden was a draw. The second match witnessed the lions collapsing under the weight of Brazil when Brazil inflicted a convincing and clinical win of three goals to zero. The last match was more disastrous when Russia sealed the fate of the lions by crushing her 6 goals to one. The lions, were therefore, shown the door of exit to quit the World Cup in America. The early defeat and exit of the lions contrary to what they performed in Italy in 1990 raised many questions from the public.

As a matter of fact, the World Cup bonanza in America received a lot of publicity. The radio gave birth to a program, *Bonjour l'Amerique* which acted "as a forum for the expression of popular support for the national team and consisted of journalistic commentary, interviews with invited guest and reports by CRTV special correspondents from the United States"(Bea Vidacs,1998). It turned out to be really a drop from sublime to ridiculous and one of the plausible reasons could be blamed on politics and politics of belonging. The political tempo had continued after the 1990 World Cup leading to the first multi party elections in Cameroon in 1992.In that election, there was massive rigging and the ruling regime used state money as usual to carry out political campaigns and at the end of the day it hung unto victory, while the SDF chairman who felt that his party was cheated declared himself the winner. This explains why the team was first and foremost in a financial quagmire in the America. By 7th July 1994 the additional fund had raised 446,317,253 FCFA (*Cameroon Tribune*, 1994).

The public was not at ease with the way things had turned out and the government in order to smoke screened the whole exercise set up a press conference in CRTV to clarify certain top issues. The Head of State special envoy to the United States, Professor Augustine Kontchou Koumegni was to be interviewed by two journalists-Justin Ndjomatuoa and Ndoutoumou, all Francophones and workers of the government's own CRTV (*Cameroon Tribune*, 1994). According to professor Kontchou Cameroon had been prematurely removed from the competition but, however, remained a great football nation. He further posit that from past records, the lions had won two African Nations cup titles and emerged finalist several times; won the Afro Asian intercontinental trophy and landed several editions of the African club winners and champions club cups. Finally, the minister consoled himself with the fact that the lions had been out in three world cups and each time it has become the darling of the people and that was why the International press and community was out in America specifically to watch the lions play. The fact that Professor Kontchou was interviewed by journalist, all of whom were Francophones and that only the government state own radio sponsored the interview did not make things serious in the least. It further showed belonging in the media and by extension sports and football in particular. (For more on the politics of belonging and media see Nyamnjoh, 2005)

However, the public was ready to hear and understand what went wrong with the Indomitable Lion's additional fund. According to Professor Kontchou, as at 7 July 1994 the sum of 446,317,253 FCFA have been contributed into the lions' fund. On the same day, a total of 420,748,000 FCFA had been spent on the lions, while 9,410,851 FCFA had been taken up as bank charges giving a balance of 16,218,402 FCFA. Unpaid bills totalling 2,105,000 FCFA and the sum of 9,598,040 FCFA were yet to be cashed. In all, the operation was yet to be over since from the total 219,009,158 FCFA announced as collection from all ten provinces, 140 million Francs were still expected to be channelled into the national account from some provinces. In effect, the Far North, North West and Centre Provinces were yet to channel their contributions to Yaoundé (*Cameroon Tribune*, 1994).

What the minister said appeared at face value to be true since the CRTV had got expertise in misinforming the public rather than really educating the public on the truth. It also appeared that he was giving the press conference when the competition was still going on which is not true. The fact that the money never reached the players in the U.S. as it was widely rumoured has remained up till date a matter of speculation. Some schools hold very strongly that the money did not reach the players and that was why the players and even the coach scattered into different directions rather than coming home in one piece. It has been very difficult to proof that assertion. Yet, it is true that many players and the coach disappeared to different directions.

The situation of the coach needs an additional attention because it is around him that the wheel of the politics of belonging rotated. After listing his twenty three men squad to take to the U.S., government officials brought untold pressure to bear on the coach to drop some of the players and take others. All these were not that those who were to be dropped could not play but rather it was because they were from a particular ethnic background. Those who were to be taken were those from areas that showed ethnic loyalties to the regime. It was because of this politics of belonging that the coach from the start made wrong choice depending on the government officials. Yet, in the press conference, the Minister of State spent his energy and people's time saying that no pressure was brought to bear on the coach about the choice of players. He, nonetheless, blamed the lion's failure on tribalism.

The history of the government, intervening in the national team with regards to the choice of players has been commonplace over the years, especially since the 1990s. Some of the players who were dropped at the 11th hour reacted ungentlemanly like Jean Claude Pagal, a skilful midfielder who was rumoured that he only knew a few minutes to the flight from Paris to Washington that he had been dropped reacted by slapping the coach. In a related vein, Ndip Akem a solid defender of the national team was dropped perhaps because he was an Anglophone and was later on transported to the U.S. to join the squad. To make sure that it was not only an Anglophone Mfede Louis Paul was asked to join the squad too. All these points to the pressure the government officials placed on the coach and the technical bench of the team. In 2004, during the African Nations' Cup in Cairo, the President of the Republic signed a decree demanding Patrick Mboma, an attacker *per excellence* to join the squad in Egypt. The coach had not earlier selected him. All said and done, the national team had scored spectacular victories and brought fame to the nation for quite some time but what is embarrassing is whether one can locate that fame. The where about of the football fame is the next issue which the paper will attempt to unravel.

### Where is the Football Fame?
The victories of the Lions give the impression rightly or wrongly that there is much in Cameroon about football fame. That might be the thought of any stranger coming into Cameroon. However, the truth is in the contrary. The first thing that catches the eye in this

football loving nation is the nature of the stadia. Cameroon has two major stadia, which were constructed in 1972 to host the African Cup of Nations ever to be hosted by Cameroon. The rest of the playing grounds are in a deplorable state and needed the intervention of FIFA before the Ahmadu Ahidjo's Stadium was renovated under the close supervision of its officials. Most of the playing grounds around the country are conterminous to pig sty. The moot question has been where the money gotten from the victories has gone to? This appears like a multi-million question which cannot be answered in the Cameroon situation which has romanced with corruption for more than two decades.

The next "fame" has been the tug of war that has been going on between the FECAFOOT and the Ministry of Youths and Sports. These two bodies, charged with the running and organisation of sports in general and the football in particular, had not militated in the interest of football in Cameroon. Instead, they are always at loggerheads because of the financial resources which they want to get access into. The ministry always wants to have a say over the finances and most of the time the Director always has to toe the line or else face immediate dismissal.

Temporal nationhood has remained for a long time the fame of all these victories. As long as the National team is playing and winning all the differences between different ethnic groups and political parties are buried. Anybody can remove his shoes and squat in the parlour of any Cameroonian who has a television to transmit images of the match. Cameroonians are well noted for their sense of forging the nation, ignorantly when football competitions are going on and it is apt to say that nationhood is attained temporarily.

Closely related to this is the constant use of football for political gains by the ruling regime. The regime has been mixing the victories of the lions with politics. And besides, football especially the elite division 1 has been politicised. In 1993, there was a plan nationwide strike by the Cameroonian civil servants ahead of the qualifier match between the lions of Cameroon and the Zimbabwean national team. The visiting Zimbabwe team was defeated and Biya declared Monday a public holiday. The strike died off. This strike had been planned by the civil servants for the government to ameliorate their financial situation. The government used the football victory to turn the scales and as a result the strike died a natural death. In 1990, the lions defeated Argentina in their opening match while the president of the Republic was there. The presence of the president in the field surmounted the political tensions that were bedevilling Cameroon with the formation of SDF, the only strong opposition party in the country at the time. Besides, whenever, the Lions win a match, the players have the prestige of being received in the presidential palace. This shows that the government is gives football a place of pride in the country. All the trophies won are paraded on the streets of the capital and provincial capitals. All these mean that the victory of the national team is a victory of the regime, particularly autocratic regimes short of tangible successes in Africa South the Sahara who try their best to channel support from sports to politics (Mehler, 2002:12). The case of Cameroon is just one of them.

At the level of Division 1 politics is reflected mostly on the day of the finals of the Cup of Cameroon. The two teams are opportune to shake hands with the head of state which is nothing more than prestige. Like Mehler (2002) one can see that football in particular comes with prestige and legitimacy in Cameroon.

Finally, the victories of the Lions and some key Division 1 teams have remained in the *imaginaire* of most Cameroonians. One can only quickly hear Cameroonians talking about the Indomitable Lions of the 1990; the Indomitable Lions of 1982; the Indomitable Lions of the victory years. This means that most of the Cameroonians look back to their victories with nostalgia at a time when it is difficult to grasp a victory. The national team is starved of victory and this could easily be explained in political terms. Cameroon has one of the best players playing in first divisions in Europe. Unfortunately, these players cannot find themselves access to the national team because of politics and belonging. If victory escaped the Lions the reasons could quickly be found in the way to which domestic politics has fluctuated over the years. Since 1990, the regime has specialised in electioneering rigging, disenfranchising a cross section of her citizens and for more than four presidential elections the incumbent has remained *in situ*. The fortunes of victory which have deserted Cameroon in continental and world competitions can also be seen in the dwindling fortunes in political arenas.

It is a truism that with all the victories and trophies won, Cameroon has hosted the African Cup of Nation's tournament only once. One would have expected that with the victories, the country could go in for a bid to host any of the tournaments. Unfortunately, there is a lot of apathy to the whole show as even now there is no hope that Cameroon will go in for a bid to host the prestigious tournament before 2015. Where does the fame lie? The Lions would have shown their fame by hosting even one tournament of the African Cup of Nations. The inability to bid for the competition can be explained on grounds that the present regime is satisfied with the victories and therefore need not worry about further victories. But that will only be to tell half the story. The present regime is so befuddled in corruption that it does not seem to understand and comprehend what her citizens really want. Everything is falling apart and the centre cannot hold anything. The state has remained for sometime a failed state and needs concrete reforms and structures to be put in place before football could have another place to breathe again.

## Conclusion

Football which initially is a genre of sports for leisure was introduced in Cameroon in the early 1920s by the African migrants. By 1959 an umbrella organisation was formed and charged with the organisation of the team sports in the country. Two years later Cameroon gained independence and by 1962, Cameroon joined the World Football Association (FIFA). Since the mid 1970s, football has ceased to become a sport for mere leisure to politics of belonging in Cameroon and the government has taken football up as a tool to manipulate the state. Current scholarship shows that the politics of belonging as suggested in current literature sprang up in the 1990s when political pundits had no true and attractive political agenda that could lure the electorate. Drawing from experiences and the archival sources, the paper defends the position that the politics and politics of belonging is well entrenched in football in Cameroon, an aspect which the extant literature has not given adequate attention. The paper further contends that victory has escaped the lions' Den because the ruling regime has decided to take up the Lions to mean many things in politics. The Indomitable Lions have therefore become euphemistic. The lack of victory in the recent competitions and the failure of the Lions even to defeat the Egyptian National team in her own backyard make it incumbent on the government to start charting a new path for football in Cameroon. It is only by charting that path and steering clear of political gymnasts that Cameroon by any iota can reclaim her lost prestige.

# Bibliography

Abdelrahman, M., 2000. *State Civil Society Relations: The politics of Egyptian NGOs*, Ph.D Dissertation, ISS, The Hague.

Ansu-Kyeremen, K. (ed) 1998. *Indigenous Communication in Africa: Concept,Application and Prospects* Ghana: Ghana University Press.

Aluko, M.A. 2003. Post colonial manipulations of ethnic diversity in Nigeria. *Identity, Cul-ture and Politics: An Afro-Asian Dialogue*, 4(1): 73-84.

Amutabi, M. 2002."The Role of Traditional Music in the Writing of Cultural History: The case of the Abaluyia of Western Kenya" In Toyin Falola and Christian Jennings (eds).*Africanising Knowledge: African Studies across the disciplines*. New Brunswick,N.J.: Transaction Publishers.

Ardener, S. ,1975. *Perceiving Women*. London: Cambridge University Press.

Arena, J.C. 1970. *The International Boundaries of Nigeria: The Framework of an Emergent African Nation*. London: Longman.

Arene, J. and Godfrey B. 1966. *Africa in the Nineteenth and Twentieth Century*. Ibadan, Nigeria: Ibadan University Press, 1966.

Arrigo, L.G. 1986. "Landownership Concentration in China: The Buck Survey Revisited" *Modern China*, vol.12,no.3:259-360.

Asiwaju, A. 1. (ed) 1985. *Partitioned Africans: Ethnic Relations AcrossAfrica's International Boundaries 1884-1984*. Lagos: University Press.

Aston, T.H. and C.Philpin,(eds) 1986. *The Brenner Debate: Agrarian Class Structure and Economic Development in Pre-industrial Europe*. Cambridge: Cambridge University Press.

Ateh, M. 1979, "On the Meaning of *Iwu Kom Tual:* An Examination of the Kom Meaning of Being and the Three Kom Hands" A Dissertation Presented in Partial Fulfilment of the Requirements for the Bachelor's Degree in Philosophy to Regional Major Seminary, Bambui, Cameroon-Affiliate of the Urban University, Rome.

Awasom, S. Y., 2005. 'The Vicissitudes of Cameroon Civil Society in the 1990s.What Lessons for the Central African Region?', in E.S.D Fomin and J.W. Forje,eds. *Central Africa: Crises, Reform and Reconstruction*, Dakar: CODESRIA.

Awasom, N.F. 2003. Anglophone/francophone identities and inter-group relations in Cameroon. In (R.T. Akinyele, *ed.*) *Race, Ethnicity and Nation-building in Africa: Stud-ies in Inter-group Relations*. Rex Charles Publications, Ibadan.

Bahl, V. 2000. "Situating and Rethinking Studies for Writing Working Class History" in Arif Dirlik, Vinay Bahl and Peter Gran (eds)*History after the Three Worlds: Post-Eurocentric Historiographies*, Maryland: Rowman and Littlefield Publishers.

Bayart, J. F., 1993. *The State in Africa: The Politics of the Belly*, London: Longman.

Bayart, J.-F. 1993. *The State in Africa: The Politics of the Belly*. Longman, London: New York.

Barongo, Y.R. 1983. "Alternative approaches to African politics". In R.B. Yolau, (ed). *Political Science in Africa: A Critical Review*, pp. 140- 153. Zed Press: London.

Bianco, L.1986. "Peasant Movements" in J.K. Fairbank and A. Feuerwerker (eds) *The Cambridge History of China*, vol.13.

Bottomore, T.B. 1976. *Elites and Society*. Middlesex, Penguin.

Bawden, M. G. and Lagdale-Brown I. (eds.)1962, An Aerial Photographic Reconnaissance of the Present and Possible Land use in the Bamenda Area, Southern Cameroons. Department of Technical Cooperation: Directorate of Overseas Surveys, Forestry Land Use.

Bratton M., 1989. "Beyond the State: Civil Society and Associational Life in Africa", *World Politics*, Vol. 43, No. 3, pp. 407-430.

Braudel, F. 1969. *Ecris sur L'Histoire*. Flammanon, Paris.

Breton,R.1983. More than 300 Languages in Cameroon. *The Courier*. 80 (July/August): 92-95.

Boggs,S.W. 1940. *International Boundaries: A Study of Boundary Functions*. New York: Academic Press.

Buijtenhuijs, R. 1978. "The revolutionary potential of black Africa: Dissident elites". *African Perspectives*: 135-147.

Carothers, T, 2000. "Civil Society - The Key to Political Economic and Societal Success?" *Deutschland*, 5 October/November: 12-17.

Ceesay, O., 1998. "State and Civil Society in Africa", *Quest*, Vol. XII, No. 1, pp 123-130.

Chabal, P., 1994. *Political Domination in Africa: Reflections on the Limits of Power,* Cam-bridge: Cambridge University Press.

Chazan, N., R. Mortimer, J. Ravenhill & D. Rothchild 1992. *Politics ami Society in Contem-porary Africa.* Lynne Rienner Publishers, Boulder: Westview

Che-Mfombong,W. 1980. "Bamenda Division Under British Administration, 1916-1961: From Native Administration to Local Government" M.A. Thesis, University of Yaounde.

Chilver, E. and P.M. Kaberry, 1967a. *Traditional Bamenda: The Pre-Colonial History and Ethnography of the Bamenda Grassfields,* vol. 1. Buea, Cameroon: Government Printing Press.

Chilver, E. 1967b. "The Kingdom of Kom in West Cameroon" In Daryll Forde and P.M. Kaberry (eds.) *West African Kingdoms in the Nineteenth Century.* Oxford: Oxford University Press.

Clignet, R. and Stark, M.1974. "Modernisation and Football in Cameroon," *Journal of Modern African Studies* 12,(9):58-72.

Comaroff, L. and Comaroff, J., eds, 1999. *Civil Society and the Political Imagination in Africa,* Chicago: Chicago University Press.

Cooper, F. 1994, 1994. "Conflict and Connection: Rethinking Colonial African History" *The American Historical Review,* vol.99, No.5

Coplan, D. 1997. "Eloquent Knowledge: Lesotho Migrants songs and the anthropology of experience" In Karin Barber (ed) *Reading in African Popular culture.* Bloomington: Indiana University Press.

Curtin, P. Steven, F. Leonard, T. and Jan, V. 1989, *African History.* Oxford, Oxford University Press.

Delancey, W.M. 1974. Plantation and migration in the Mt. Cameroon region. In H.F. Illy, (ed) *Kamerun: Strukturen und Probleme der Soziookonomischen Entwicklung.* von J-lase & Koehler, Mainz.

de Vries, J. 1998. *Catholic Mission, Colonial Government and Indigenous Response in Kom (Cameroon)* Leiden: African Studies Centre.

De Oliveira, M. D. and Tandon, R., 1994. An Emerging Global Civil Society', in S.Myers, ed., *Democracy Is a Discussion,* Connecticut: Toor Commings Center.

Cherniavsky, E. 1996. "Subaltern Studies in a U.S. Frame" *Boundary* Vol.23,no.2:85-110.

Ergene, B.A. 1998. "Subalternity ,postcolonial Critique and the Ottoman peasantry: A Critical evaluation of the modern approaches to Ottoman state-society relations" *Critique Fall:* 29-43. Falola,T. and Christain Jennings (eds.), 2002, *Africanizing Knowledge: African Studies Across Disciplines.* New Brunsuwick, N.J.: Transaction Publishers, pp.191-207.

Fanso, V.G. 1989. *Cameroon History for Secondary Schools and Colleges Vol. 1: Pre-historic Times to the Nineteenth Century.* London: Macmillan.

Fanso, V.G.1983. "Trans-Frontier Relations and Resistance to

Cameroon-Nigeria Colonial Boundaries, 1916-1945" PhD Thesis, University of Yaounde.

Fanso, V.G._1989. *Cameroon History for Secondary Schools andColleges Vol. 2: From Colonial to Post Colonial Periods.* London: Macmillan.

Fatton Jr., R., 1995, Africa in the Age of Democratisation: The Civic Limitations of Civil Society', *African Studies Review,* Vol. 38, No. 2, pp. *72-77.*

Feierman, S. 1990. *Peasant Intellectuals: Anthropology and History in Tanzania.* Wisconsin: University of Wisconsin Press.

Finnegan, R.1970.*Oral Literature in Africa.* Oxford: Oxford University Press.

Fochingong, C.C. 2004. The travails of democratization in Cameroon in the context of politi-cal liberalisation since the 1990s. *African and Asian Studies,* 3(1): 33-59.

Fochingong, T.N. 1998. Multipartism and demoralisation in Cameroon.*Journal of Third World Studies,* 15(2): 119-136.

Forde, Darlyll and Kaberry P.M. (eds.). 1967. *West African Kingdoms in the Nineteenth Century.* Oxford: Oxford University Press,

Forje, J.W., 2003, 'Rethinking Social Responsibility and Governance for Sustainability: Lessons from Developing Polities in Africa', *Journal of Applied Social,* Vol. 3, No. 1:444.

Freud, B. 1998. *The Making of Contemporary Africa: The Development of African Society since 1800.* Boulder, Colorado: Lynne Rienner.

Fukui, K. and Markatis J. (eds.) 1993. *Ethnicity and Conflict in the Horn of Africa.* Athens: Ohio University Press.

Gam, O. 1997, "A Pastoral Approach to Conflict Resolution" M.A. Dissertation (Theology) St. Thomas Aquinas Major Seminary Bambui, Affiliate of the Pontifical Urban University, Rome.

Geschier P. 2001. Issues of citizenship and belonging in present-day Africa. In (L.Kropacek and P.Skalnik (eds) *Africa 2000: Forty Years of African Studies in Prague*.:Prague:Set out.

Geschiere,P.. and Nyamnjoh, B 1999."Capitalism and Autothony: The seesaw mobility and belonging. In (J.Comaroff and J.L.Comaroff (eds) *Millenial Capitalism and the Culture of Neo-liberalism*. London: Zed Books.

Geschiere, P. 2009. *The perils of belonging: Autochtony, Citizenship, and exclusion in Africa and Europe*, Chicago: University of Chicago Press.

Geschiere, P., 2004. Ecology, belonging and xenophobia: The 1994 Forest Law in Cameroon and the issue of community. In (H. Englund & F. Nyamnjoh, *(eds) Rights and the Politics of Recognition in Africa*, pp. 237-259. /ed Books, London.

Ghali, B.B. and Asfahany, N. 1973. *Les conflits cles Frontieres en Afriquc*. Paris : Etudes et Documents.

Gifford, P., 1997. *African Christianity: Its Public Role*, London: Hurst.

Gopal,P. 2004. "Reading Subaltern history" in Neil Lazarus (ed) *The Cambridge Companion to Postcolonial Literacy Studies*. Cambridge:Cambridge University Press.

Gramsci, A.1973. *Selections from the Prison Notebooks*. New York: International Publishers.

Guha, R. and Gayatri,C.S.(eds),1989. *Selected Subaltern Studies*. New York: Oxford University Press.

Guha, R. 1989. "On Some aspects of the Historiography of Colonial India", in Guha Ranajit and Gayatri Spivak (eds) *Selected Subaltern Studies*.Oxford: Oxford University Press: 37-44

Guya, R., and Gayatri, S.C.; 1988. *Selected Subaltern Studies*. Oxford: Oxford University Press.

Harbeson, J. W, David, R. and Naomi C, eds., 1994. *Civil Society and the State in Africa*, Boulder: Lynne Reinner.

Harneit-Sievers, A.; Jones O. Ahazuem and Sydney Emezue, 1997. (eds) *A Social History of the Nigerian Civil War. Perspectives from Below*. Enugu and Hamburg: Jemezei Associates and LIT Verlag.

Harneit-Seivers, A., 2000. (ed) *A Place in the World: New Local Historiographies from Africa and South Asia* .Leiden: Brill.

Hartshorne, L. 1938. *A Study of the Boundary Problems of Europe*. Cambridge: Cambridge University Press.

Hay, M.J. and Stichter, S. (eds.). 1984. *African Women South of the Sahara*. London: Cambridge University Press,

Holdich, T. 1976. *Political Frontiers and Boundary Making*. London: Longman

Holm, J.D., Moluts P. P and Somolekae, G., 1996. "The Development of Civil Society in a Democratic State. The Botswana Model", *African Studies Review,*Vol. 39, No. 2, pp. 43-69.

Horst, A. Horst and Daniel M. 2006. *The Cell Phone: An Anthropology of Communication* Oxford: Oxford University Press.

Hussain, A. 1973. "The educated elite: Collaborators, assailants, nationalists. A note on African nationalists and nationalism". *Journal of the Historical Society of Nigeria*. 7(1): 485-497.

Ihonvbere, J.O.1994. "Africa in the 1990s and beyond: Alternative prescriptions and projections and projections" *Science Direct*, vol.28, No.1 (1996):15-35.

Iliffe, J. 1987. *The African Poor: a history*. Cambridge: Cambridge University Press.

Isumonah, V.A. 2001. Oil-bearing minorities struggles in Nigeria: Towards an alternative constitutional framework. *Journal of the Indian Law Institute* 43(2): 174-190.

Johnson, W.B. 1970. *The Cameroon Federation: Political Integration in a Fragmentary Society*. Prince-ton University Press, Princelon.

Joseph, R., 1978. 'Introduction and General Framework', in R. Joseph, ed., *Gaullist Africa: Cameroon under Ahmadu Ahidjo*, Enugu: Fourth Dimensions.

Joseph, R., 1998."Africa, 1990-1997:From Abertua to Closure" *Journal of Democracy*, vol.9, No.2(1998): 3-17.

Jones, S.B. 1945. *Boundary Making: A Handbook for Statesmen, Treaty Editors and Boundary Commissioners*. Washington O.C: Carnegie Endowment.

Kale, P.M. 1967. *Political Evolution in the Cameroons*. Buea: Government Printers.

Kandeh, J.2004. *Coups from Below: Armed Subalterns and State Power in West Africa*, New York: Palgrave Macmillan.

Kasfir, N., ed., 1998.*Civil Society and Democracy in Africa: Critical Perspectives,* Ilford: Frank Lass.

Ki-Zerbo, J. 1990. *General History of Africa: Methodology and Africa Pre-history* Cambridge: Cambridge University Press.

Ki-Zerbo, J. 1978.*Histoire de L'Afrique Noire:D, Hier a Demain* with a prefaceby Fernand Braudel (Paris: Hatier.

Konings, P. and Nyamnjoh, F. B., 1997. 'The Anglophone Problem in Cameroon', *Journal of Modern African Studies,* Vol. 35, No. 2, pp. 215-235

Konings, P, 2002. 'University Students Revolt, Ethnic Militia and Violence during Political Liberalisation in Cameroon', *African Studies Review,* Vol. 45, No. 2,     pp.179-204.

Konings, P. 1993. *Labour Resistance in Cameroon: Managerial Strategies and Labour Resistance in the Agro-Industrial Plantations of the Cameroon Development Corporation.* London: Oxford University Press.

Konings, P. & F. Nyamnjoh 2003. *Negotiating an Anglophone Identity: A Study of the Poli-tics of Recognition and Representation in Cameroon.* African Studies Center, Leiden.

Korvenonja, T. 1993. The environmental problems and politics of power: Review on the Afri-can elite. *Nordic Journal of African Studies,* 2(1): 140 154.

Krieger, M. 2008. *Cameroon's Social Democratic Front: Its History and Prospects as an Opposition political party, 1990-2011.* Bamenda: LANGAA RPCIP

Lalu, P.1998. "Medical Anthropology, Subaltern Traces, and the Making and Meaning of Western Medicine in South Africa: 1895-1899" *History in Africa,* Vol.25: 133-159.

Lawrence, Benjamin N.; Emily Lynn Osborn and Richard L. R.(eds) .2006. *Intermediaries, Interpreters and Clerks: African Employees in the Making of Colonial Africa* Wisconsin: The University of Wisconsin Press

Leach, M. (ed.), 1950. *Standard Dictionary of Folklore, Mythology,and Legend.* New York:   Funk and Wagnall.

LeVine,V.T. 1964. *The Cameroons from Mandate to Independence.* University of California Press, Los Angeles.

Ludden, D. (ed) 2001. *Reading Subaltern Studies. Critical History Contested Meaning and the Globalisation of South Asia.* London: Oxford University Press.

Mallon, F.E. 1994."The Promise and Dilemma of Subaltern Studies: Perspectives from Latin American History", *American Historical Review*, vol.99:1491-1515.

Mamdani, M.1996, *Citizenship and Subject: Contemporary Africa and the Legacy of Late Colonialism*.London:James and Currey.

Mamdani, M., 1995, A Critique of the State and Civil Society Paradigm in Africanist Studies', in M. Mamdani and E. Wamba-dia- Wamba, eds. *African Studies in Social Movements and Democracy*. Dakar: CODESRIA.

Mamdani, M., 1998. *When Does a Settler Become a Native? Reflections of the Colonial Roots of Citizenship in Equatorial and South Africa*. Inaugural lecture as A.C. Jordan Professor of African Studies, University of Cape Town, 13 May 1998.

Mazrui, A. 1969. "Africa's Exploration and Africa's Self-Discovery," *Journal of Modern African Studies*, vol.7, No.4: 661-676.

Mbi, J. T. 2004.*Ecclesia in Africa is US: An Attempt at Liturgical Inculturation for the Ecclesiastical Province of Bamenda*. Yaounde, Cameroon: Impression AMA-CENC.

Mbile, N.N. 2000. *Cameroon Political Story: Memories of an Authentic Eyewitness*. Presbook, Limbe.

Mboukou, A. 1981. "The rise of anti-intellectualism among the modern African elite". *Journal of African Studies, 8(1): 180-186*.

Milne, M. 1999. No *Telephone to Heaven: From Apex to Nadir – Colonial Service in Nigeria, Aden, the Cameroons and Gold Coast, 1938- 1961*. London: Meon Hill Press.

Mitchell, L.J.2002. Traces in the Landscape: Hunters, Herders and Farmers on the Cedarberg Frontier, South Africa, 1725-95" *The Journal of African History*, Vol.43, and No.3:431-450.

Moore, D.S. 1998." Subaltern Struggles and the Politics of Place: Remapping Resistance in Zimbabwe's Eastern Highlands" *Cultural Anthropology*, Vol.13, and No.3: 344-381.

Mphahlele, E. 1959. *The dilemma of the African elite. The Twentieth Century* 1959 (April): 319-325.

Merriam, A.R. 1967. "The Use of Music as a Technique of Reconstructing Culture History in Africa" In Creighton Gabel and Nordman R. Bennett (eds) *Reconstructing African Culture History*, Boston, Mass.: Boston University Press.

Mbuagbo, O. T. and Fru, C.N., 2003. "Civil society and Democratisation: The Cameroonian Experience", *Journal of Social Development in Africa*, Vol. 18, No.2:133-149.

Mbuagbo, O. T, and Robert, M. A., 2004, 'Roll-Back: Democratisation and Social Fragmentation in Cameroon', *Nordic Journal of African Studies*, Vol. 13, No. 1:1-12.

Mehler, A.2002. Football in Africa: Are the Democratic Lions about to Take Over? *News from the Nordik Africa Institute*.No.3:12-13.

Mkandawire, T. and Adebayo O., eds., 1995. *Between Liberalisation and Oppression: Vie Politics of Structural Adjustment in Africa*, Dakar: CODESRIA.

Monga, C., 1998.*The Anthropology of Anger: Civil society and Democracy in Africa*, London: Lynne Rienner.

Morton, M. 2007. *Gayatri Spivak, Ethics, Subalternity and Critique of post colonial reason*. London: Polity Press.

Murdock, 1959. *Africa: Its Peoples and their Culture History*. New York: MacGraw Hill.

Ndembiyembe, P. C., 1997.'Pressent tribalisme au Cameroun', in Gerddes, C., (ed.), *La democratic a l'epreuve du tribalisme*, Yaounde: Saagraph, pp. 49-57.

Ngoh, V.J. 2001. *Southern Cameroons,1922-1961: A Constitutional History*. Burlington: Ashgate.

Ngoh, V. J. 1996. *History of Cameroons Since 1800*. Limbe: Presbook.

Ngoh, V.J. 2004. "Biya and the Transition to Democracy", In John Mukum Mbaku and Joseph Takougang (eds) *The Leadership Challenge in Africa: Cameroon Under Paul Biya*. Boulder, Colarado: Westview Press.

Ngwa, J.A. 1988. *An Outline Geography of the United Republic of Cameroon*. London: Longman, 1988.

Nkwi, Paul N. and Vidacs, B.1997."Football: Politics and Power in Cameroon" In G.Armstrong and R.Guilianotti(eds) *Entering the Field: New Perspectives in World Football*.: London: Oxford.

Nkwi, Paul N. 1976. *Traditional government and Social Change: A Study of the Political Institutions among the Kom of Cameroon Grassfields*. Fribourg: Fribourg University Press.

Nkwi, Paul N. and J.P. W.1982. *Elements for a History of the Western Grassfields:* Yaounde: Department of Social and Anthropology, University of Yaounde.

Nkwi, Paul N. 1987.*Traditional Diplomacy: A Study of Inter- Chiefdom Relations in the Western Grassfields, North West Province of* Cameroon. Yaounde: University of Yaounde Press.

Nkwi, W.G. 2009(e). "Football and the politics of belonging in contemporary Cameroon, c.1979-2004: A Historical meditation" *Journal of Applied Social Sciences: a Multidisciplinary Journal of the Faculty of Social and Management Sciences,* vol.8, No.1 and 2: 119-139

Nkwi, W.G. 2009 (d)."The *Afo-a-Kom,* Civil Society and Governance amongst the Kom and Her Neighbours, C.1865-1973" in Tangie Nsoh Fonchingong and John Bobuin Gemandze (eds) *Cameroon: The Stakes and Challenges of Governance and Development.* Mankon, Bamenda: *Langaa* Research and Publishing Common Initiative Group.

Nkwi, W.G.2009(c)"From Elitist to the voice of Commonality of voice communication: The Social History of Telephone in Buea, Cameroon" in *Telephone and Cell Phone in Africa and Beyond* Mankon, Bamenda: Langaa Research and Publishing Common Initiative Group.

Nkwi, W.G.2009 (b) "Review of African Hidden Histories edited by Karin Barber" *Journal of African Affairs* , Vol.108, No.431(April 2009): 325-326.

Nkwi, W.G. 2009(a) with Victor Julius Ngoh and Kah Henry Kam: "Bimbia and its Environs in the Trans-Atlantic Slave Trade" in Einer Neimi og Christine Smith-Simonsen (RED.*) DET HJEMLIGE OG DET GLABSLE:FESTSKRIFT TIL RANDI RONNING BALSVIK* (Oslo,Norway: Akademisk Publisering, 2009):155-171.

Nkwi, W.G.2008."The voice of the voiceless": Telephone and telephone operators in Anglophone Cameroon. *epasa moto:A Bilingual Journal of arts, Letters and the Humanities,* vol.,3 No.2 (December 2008) :187-206.

Nkwi, W.G.2007(b)"Boundary Conflicts in Africa: The Case of Bambili and Babanki-Tungoh, of Northwest Cameroon, c.1955-1998" *Journal of Applied Social Science: A Multidisciplinary Journal of the Faculty of Social and Management Sciences,*Vol.6,Nos.1and 2:6-41.

Nkwi, W.G. 2007 (a)"The Anglophone Problem in Cameroon: Towards New insights" in Pierre Fandio and Mongi Madini (eds) *Figures de L'histoire et Imaginaire au Cameroun: Actors of History and Artistic Creativity in Cameroon* (Paris: L, Harmattan, 2007) pp.153-160

Nkwi, W.G. 2006 (c), "Elites, Ethno-Regional Competition in Cameroon, and the Southwest Elites Association (SWELA), 1991-1997."*African Study Monographs,* 27(3):123-143.

Nkwi, W.G.2006 (b) "Folk-songs and History amongst the Kom of Northwest Cameroon: The Pre-colonial and Post Colonial Periods" *Humanities Review Journal,* vol.6:62-76.

Nkwi, W.G. 2006(a) "The Dilemma of Civil Society in Cameroon Since 1990: Which way forward?" *African Journal of International Affairs,* vol.9, Nos.1&2:91-106.

Nkwi, W.G. 2005. "From Village to National and Global Art: Whose art?"In E.S.D. Fomin and Foje W. John(eds.) *Central Africa – Crises and Reconstruction* (Dakar, CODESRIA, 2005):133-154

Nkwi,W.G.2004."The Anglophone Problem" In Victor Julius Ngoh(ed.) *Cameroon: From a Federal to a Unitary State, 1961-1972: A Critical Study* .Limbe Cameroon: Design House: 185-209.

Nkwi, W .G. 2003. "The Political Activities of *Anlu* in the British Southern Cameroons Politics, 1958-1961: The case of Kom Fondom" *Epasamoto: A Bilingual Journal of Arts, Letters and the Humanities.* Vol.1, No 6 (2003): 154-175

Nyamnjoh, F.B. 1997. 'Media, Tribalism and Democracy in Cameroon, in Gerddes, C, ed., *La democratic a l'epreuve du tribalisme,* Yaounde: Saagraph, pp. 59-80.

Nyamnjoh, F. 1997. *Political rumour in Cameroon.* Cahier de l'UCA, *2: 93-106.*

Nyamnjoh, F. B., 1999.'Cameroon: a Country United by Ethnic Ambition and Difference', *African Affairs,* Vol. 98, No. 390, pp. 104-125.

Nyamnjoh, F. B. and Rowlands, M., 1998, 'Elite Associations and the Politics o f Belonging in Cameroon', *Africa,* Vol. 68, No.3, pp. 321-337.

Nyamnjoh, F. B.2005. *Africa's Media: Democracy and the Politics of Belonging* .London: Zed Books.

Nyamnjoh, B. and Rowlands, M..1998. "Elite Associations and the Politics of Belonging in Cameroon." *Africa,* 68(3):320-337.

Nyamnjoh, F. B. 2005. *Africa's Media: Democracy and the Politics of Belonging* London: ZED Press.

Nyamnjoh, F.B.1998. "Indigenous Means of Communication in Cameroon" In T. R. World(ed) *Telecoms in Africa: From Tat am to Internet.* Johannesburg and Houghton.

Oben, T. and Akoko,M.2004."Motions of support and ethno regional politics in Cameroon." *Journal of Third World Studies*, 111(1):241-258.

O'Donnel, G. and Schmitter, P. C., 1991. *Transitions from Authoritarian Rule: Tenta-tive Conclusions about Uncertain Democracies*, Baltimore: John Hopkins Univer-sity Press.

O'Neil, Robert (1991) *Mission to the British Cameroons*. London: Cambridge University Press.

Orkin, M., 1995. 'Building Democracy in the New South Africa: Civil Society, Citi-zenship and Political Ideology', *Review of African Political Economy*, No.66, pp. 525-537.

Osaghae, E. E., (ed), *1994. Between state and Civil Society in Africa*, Dakar: CODESRIA

Osaghae, E.E., 1998.'Rescuing the Post-Colonial State in Africa: A Re-conceptualization of the Role of Civil Society', *Quest*, Vol. XII, No. I, pp. 203-206.

Osaghae, E.E. 1991. *"A* re-examination of the conception of ethnicity of Africa as an ideology of inter-elite competition". *African Study Monographs, 12(1): 43-60.*

Pannenborg, A. 2008. *How to win a Football Match in Cameroon: An anthropological study of Africa's most popular sport.* Leiden: ASC.

Partha, C.2006. "A Brief History of Subaltern Studies", In Sebastian Conrad (ed) *Transnationale Geschihte. Themen, Tendenzen und Theorien.*Germany: Gottingen: 94-104.

Pelak, C.F. 2006. "Local-Global Processes: Linking Globalization, Democratization, and the Development Women's Football in South Africa" *Afrika Spectrum* 41:371-392.

Percival, J.2008. *The 1961 Cameroon plebiscite: Choice or betrayal. Mankon*, Bamenda: Langaa, RPCIG.

Pongweni, Alec J.C. 1997. "The Chimurenga Songs of the Zimbabwe War of Liberation". In Karin Barber (ed.) *Readings in African Popular Culture*. Bloomington: Indiana University Press.

Poggi, G., 1978.*The Development of the Modem State*, Stanford: Stanford University Press.

Priya, N.2003."Examining the undisclosed margins: Post colonial intellectuals and Subaltern voices" *Journal of Cultural Studies,* Vol. 17, No.1:56-84

Rangers, T. O.,2000. *Voices from the rocks: nature, culture and history in the Matopos Hills of Zimbabwe* Oxford: James Currey.

Rangers, T.O. 1983. "The Invention of Tradition in colonial Africa" in Eric Hobsbwam and Terence Rangers (eds) *The Invention of Tradition.* Cambridge: Cambridge University Press.

Rangers,T.O. 1985. *Peasant Consciousness and Guerilla War in Zimbabwe: A Comparative Study.* London: James Currey; Los Angeles and Berkeley: University of California Press.

Ritzenthaler, R.1961. "Anlu: A Woman's Uprising in the British Cameroons" *African Studies* vol. 3, No. 19.

Robert, A. 1988. *Photographs as sources for African History.* London: School of African and Orioental Studies.

Robinson, P.T. 1994. "The National Conference Phenomenon in Francophone Africa" *Comparative Studies in society and History*, vol.36, No.3575-610.

Rodriguez,I. (ed)2001. *The Latin American Subaltern Studies Reader.* Durham NC: Duke University Press.

Rodriguez, I.2005. "Is there a Need for Subaltern Studies?" *Disposition* Vol.52, no.25:43-63.

Rosalind, O.1998. "Recovering the Subject: Subaltern Studies and Histories of Resistance in Colonial South Asia", *Modern Asian Studies.* Vol.22, No.1:189-224

Rudin, H. 1938. *Germans in the Cameroons, 1884-1914: A case study in Modem Imperialism* Yale: Yale University Press.

Rudolph, S. 1987. "State Formation in Asia ". *Journal of Asian Studies.* Vol.46, no.4: 731-746.

Ryder, R.1970 "Traditions and History" in J.D.Fage(ed) *Africa Discovers Her Past* London: Oxford University Press.

Sarkar, S.1997. "The Decline of the Subaltern in Subaltern Studies" in Chaturvedi (eds) *Writing Social History.* Delhi: Oxford University Press: 82-108.

Scott, J. 1976. *The Moral Economy of the Peasant.* New Haven: Yale University Press.

Scott.J.1985. *Weapons of the Weak: Everyday Forms of Peasant Resistance.* New Haven:Yale University Press.

Scott, J. 1990. *Domination and the arts of Resistance: Hidden Transcripts*. New Haven: Yale University Press.

Searl, J. 1995. *The Construction of Social Reality*. Penguin, London.

Shanklin, E.1976. "The Odyssey of *Afo-a-kom" Africa Arts, vol.* l, No.23.

Sitoe, E., 1998.'State and Civil Society in Africa: An Instance of Asymmetric In-terdependence', *Quest,* Vol. XII, No.l, pp. 203-216.

Sklar, R., 1987.'Developmental Democracy', *Comparative Studies in Society and His-tory,* Vol. 29, No.4, pp. 686-714.

Schatzberg, M. 2006."Soccer, Science, and Sorcery: Causation and African Football" *Afrika Spectrum 41*:351-369.

Smith, D J. 2006. "Cell Phones, Social Inequality and Contemporary Culture in Nigeria'" *Canadian Journal of African Studies* vol.40, No.3:497-523.

Tanga, S. 1969. Le Football Camerounaise des Origins a l'independence. Yaounde.

Takougang, J. and Krieger, M., 1998. *African State and Society in the 1990s: Cameroon's Political Crossroads,* Boulder: Westview Press.

Vail, L. and Landeg W.1997." Plantation Protest: The history of a Mozambican song" In Karin Barber (ed.) *Readings in African Popular Culture*. Bloomington: Indiana University Press.

van den Lindfors, B. 1974. "Popular literature for African elite". *Journal of Modern African Studies,* 12(3): 471-484.

Vansina,V.1985. *Oral Tradition as History* .London: James Currey.

Vansina,V.1980. "Memory and Oral Tradition" in Joseph C.Miller(ed.) *The African pasts speaks: Essays on Oral Tradition and history*. Connecticut: Shoe String Press.

Verdesio,G.(ed). 2005. Latin American Subaltern Studies Revisited. *Special issue of Dispositio/Disposition*. Vol.25, no.52

Wallerstein, E. *1965. Elites in French-speaking West Africa: The social basis of ideas. The Journal of Modern African Studies,* 3: *1-2.*

Wamba-dia-Wamba, E. 1992. *Beyond elite politics of democracy in Africa*. Quest VI, *1: 29-42.*

Williams, G. 2002.*The other side of the Popular: Neoliberalism and subalternity in Latin America*. Duke: Duke University Press.

Williams, R.J. 2006. "Doing History": Nurudin Farah's Sweet and Sour Milk Subaltern Studies and the Post colonial Trajectory of Silence", Research in African Literatures. Vol.37, no.4: 161-176.

Wilson, J. 1981. *Land Tenure and State Land.* Yaounde: National Printing Press.

Wiredu, 1C, 1998.'The State, Civil Society and Democracy in Africa', *Quest,* Vol. 12, No.l, pp. 241-253.

Woods, D., 1992. 'Civil Society in Europe and Africa: Limiting State Power through a Public Sphere', *African Studies Review,* Vol. 35, No.2, pp. 77-100.

Vlastos, S. 1986. *Peasant Protests and Uprisings in Tokugawa Japan.* Berkeley: University of California Press.

Yanou, M.A. 2007. "Reunification and the eleventh province Dilemma in Cameroon", Cameroon Journal on Democracy and Human Rights (http://www.cjdhr.org) ,vol.1, No.2: 25-27.

Yenshu, E., 2001. 'Social Movements and Political Parties during the Structural Adjustment Programme in Cameroon: A Critical Survey of Some Literature', paper presented at Third World Forum, Dakar, 14-16 April.

Yenshu, E. 2006. "Management of Ethnic Diversity in Cameroon against the backdrop of Social crises", *Cahiers d'etudes africaines* vol.46, No.181 : 135-156.

Yenshu, E. 1998. "The discourse and politics of indigenous/minority political rights in some metropolitan areas of Cameroon" *Journal of Applied Social Sciences, 1(1): 25- 41.*

www.ingramcontent.com/pod-product-compliance
Lightning Source LLC
Chambersburg PA
CBHW021905020426
42334CB00013B/490